THE HOUSE OF THE DOUBLE AXE

By Agnes Carr Vaughan

THE HOUSE OF
THE DOUBLE AXE

THE PALACE AT KNOSSOS

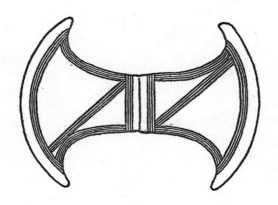

AGNES CARR VAUGHAN

PROFESSOR EMERITUS OF CLASSICAL LANGUAGES
AND LITERATURES, SMITH COLLEGE

ILLUSTRATED WITH PHOTOGRAPHS

Doubleday & Company, Inc., Garden City, New York
1959

Library of Congress Catalog Card Number 59–11613

In Memoriam
G.T.S.

Numberless are the world's wonders, but none
More wonderful than man; the stormgrey sea
Yields to his prows, the huge crests bear him high;
. . . from every wind
He has made himself secure—from all but one:
In the late wind of death he cannot stand.

SOPHOCLES

CONTENTS

11

CONTENTS

INTRODUCTION

Few modern travelers, in these breathless days of rapid transit by plane or motor car, have either the time or the opportunity to wander on foot and alone over a Greek island. A visitor from Athens to Crete can be whisked there in a matter of minutes, only seventy-five, unless his plane encounters head winds. Fifty years ago this would not have been possible. Then, like Sir Arthur Evans or his predecessor, Heinrich Schliemann, he would have arrived by slow boat, tramped the island on foot, following the goats over the high mountains and through the fertile valleys, or, astride a mule or donkey, have made his way in somewhat dubious comfort wherever he could.

The nineteenth century saw many intrepid wanderers in Crete, not all as well acquainted as Evans or Schliemann with the storied history of the island, but each one with enough in his head to fancy that wherever he set foot to the ground he might be treading on the roof of an ancient palace or temple, buried centuries ago by the accumulated debris of the past. Yet no one, historian, archaeologist, scholar, or poet, however vivid his imagination, could have credited his ears,

so far behind reality does fiction lag, had he been told that
the goods and chattels of a bygone people still lay forgotten
in the ruins of the almost legendary city of Knossos, whose
powerful sea lords, under the ancient name of Priest-King,
once held sway over the prehistoric Mediterranean world.

Evans, to whom the honor of discovering Knossos belongs,
had no way of knowing that under the great rectangular
mound, its summit thickly grown with olive trees, into which
he sank his first test pits, he would find a civilization that was
destined to become one of the sensations of the twentieth
century.

His task might have been simplified, had the modern
method been invented of testing soil with the radioactive
Carbon 14. The Carbon-14 method, applied to man-made
charcoal and used in the 1956 excavation of Russell Cave in
Alabama, showed that the cave had been inhabited for approximately 8160 years. Without such an aid Evans had recourse to the usual archaeological device of sinking test pits
and carefully measuring and recording each layer of soil. By
this method he found that Knossos had already been settled
in the Neolithic Age, the period of highly finished stone implements, or more than three thousand years before the
building of the Great Pyramid in Egypt. He found no traces
of a Paleolithic or Earlier Stone Age culture.

The unearthing of Knossos, a task that stretched over
thirty exciting, although sometimes frustrating, years, he has
set forth at length in his great work, *The Palace of Minos at
Knossos*. The enormous structure he discovered in the center
of the vast city he identified as the palace of an early empire
builder, known to the ancient world by the name of Minos,
whose daring exploits, gathering fame through the ages,
transformed him into a semi-mythical ruler with an underground labyrinth and a Minotaur. In his text Evans refers to
the palace of Minos as the "House of the Double Axe," and
today the double axe has become the symbol of that extra-

ordinary civilization which, over thirty-five hundred years ago, flourished on the island of Crete. *The House of the Double Axe* has therefore seemed a fitting title for this undertaking of mine.

Although I have not consciously designed this book to serve as a guide for either the scholar or the traveler, since they can manage well enough without it, I confess to a hope that they may find in it something of interest and perhaps of value. If the scholar finds errors of fact or interpretation and the traveler more detail than his time will allow him to absorb, the fault will be that of both omission and commission. The scholar may also take exception to the spelling of the classical names in the text. This is a matter of perennial controversy. In general, I have adopted the current usage of retaining the Greek spelling for unfamiliar names and the English spelling for familiar ones. Certain inconsistencies remain. For these I make no apology.

Frankly, however, it is that nebulous creature known as the layman for whom this book is intended. Fascinated by what he hears and often sees of buried cities that are still emerging from their graves in various parts of the world, he wants to know something of the life their inhabitants lived so long ago. Since no literature has survived from prehistoric Crete I have attempted to reconstruct from the existing monuments not only the material world of Knossos and its people but the mental and spiritual atmosphere as well. In this risky adventure I have encountered many difficulties, especially in such controversial matters as the subject of bull-grappling or the interpretation of the Minoan tablets. I have attempted to present the evidence without taking sides. I also do not want to take sides in the sometimes heated discussions over the reconstruction of the palace under Evans's direction, since scholarly opinion has always been as widely diverse as are the opinions of many who visit the site of Knossos today.

Although supplemented by other sources, both ancient

and modern, by visits to the various sites on Crete where
excavations have been conducted, and by study of the splen-
did collection in the Candia Museum in Heracleion, *The
Palace of Minos* has proved invaluable to me. Just as one is
often rude without warrant to one's friends, I have been
guilty of rudeness to Sir Arthur by not acknowledging my
indebtedness to him in footnotes. Had I done so, I should
have had to acknowledge many other authorities. Chiefly for
this reason, I have discarded all footnotes.

The actual writing of this book has been carried on in
places as remote from each other as Chile and Greece. In
Chile my kind hosts, Mr. and Mrs. Newman Romero, arranged an out-of-door studio for me under the branches of a
tree loaded with ripe apricots; in Greece the ever changing
tints of Mount Hymettus and the emerald waters of the
Saronic Gulf, both visible from my veranda, proved more dis-
tracting than the ripe apricots. I owe my rescue to the sym-
pathetic assistance of members of the American School of
Classical Studies at Athens, to the generosity of the American
Academy in Rome in allowing me the use of the library, and
to the kind helpfulness of Mr. Nicholas Platon, the able Director of the Candia Museum.

For the photographs which appear in this book I am
indebted to Virginia Garner; to Dr. M. Alison Frantz of the
American School of Classical Studies at Athens; to the
Candia Museum in Crete; and to Edward J. Moore of the
Museum of Fine Arts in Boston. I wish also to thank
Dr. Walter Haynes, Assistant Librarian of Harvard University, and Dr. Jacques Barzun, Dean of the Graduate School
of Columbia University. To Dr. John L. Caskey, the Director
of the American School of Classical Studies at Athens, and
particularly to Dr. Clara W. Crane of Bridgewater, Massachusetts, I am greatly indebted for careful and critical reading of
the manuscript and for valuable suggestions. For voluntary

secretarial assistance I owe many thanks to Mrs. Casparian of Pierce College.

Finally, I wish to take this opportunity to acknowledge my indebtedness to President Helen R. H. Nichol, who, at a dark moment in my life, gathered me into the friendly company of her faculty at Orlinda Childs Pierce College. To her unflagging interest and encouragement I owe much.

Agnes Carr Vaughan

Ellenico
Greece

PART ONE
THE GREAT DISCOVERY

CHAPTER ONE

AN ISLAND IN THE GREAT GREEN SEA

The Great Green Sea, as ancient Egyptian records called the Mediterranean, is dotted with islands all the way from Gibraltar to the Suez Canal. Some are large; others are small. In the eastern Mediterranean the largest is Crete.

Once the most prosperous, she is now one of the most barren. Her virgin forests of cypress and of cedar have almost vanished, and two thirds of the island is a stony waste. Alien peoples have swept over her; she has belonged now to this power, now to that. Time after time earthquakes have laid her low. But in spite of her many calamities, Crete has preserved her identity throughout the centuries. Phoenixlike, she has risen, shaken but triumphant, from the ashes of her earthquakes. The sun still shines strongly down upon her slopes; flowers spring up amid the rocks; and the busy hum of bees fills the air.

The Greek mainland lies to the north of Crete, the great Libyan promontory to the south, and to the east stretches the long coast of Asia. And in the near distance rises island after island, bare and rocky, yet strangely inviting, almost as though the sea had tossed them up from her green depths to act as strategic steppingstones for those Cretan mariners who early set forth upon her in their fish-tailed boats.

In time these daring adventurers returned to their island with accounts of rare things to be found in far-off lands: copper in Cyprus, the Copper Island, silver in Cilicia, the tusk of an elephant in Egypt, sawed and cut and polished until it became gleaming ivory, and gold, too, beyond imagining. They themselves had gracefully shaped pottery to offer, engraved gems, cutting tools of obsidian, and cunning hands. So Crete soon became known as a friendly place where merchants were eager for trade.

Eons ago Crete may have been connected with the Balkan Peninsula by a land bridge. No visible trace of that remains. Today the island is shaped somewhat like a parallelogram. Seen from the air, it presents the appearance of a barrier reef, with the sea dashing against its fretted coastline. Its length is about one hundred and seventy miles. At its widest part it is about thirty-five miles, at its narrowest only between seven and eight. A mountain range of dark limestone runs east and west well across the island on its long central axis. Its highest peak, known in olden days as Mount Ida, rises to a height of over eight thousand feet against the intense blue of the Cretan sky. Snow-clad until almost the middle of the summer, Mount Ida is a familiar and arresting landmark. The spurs of the limestone range enclose narrow, fertile valleys, with little or no communication between them. On the northern side they form long, slender peninsulas separated by inlets that were havens of refuge to early mariners but that also provided excellent bases for pirates.

To geographers the coastline of Crete—six hundred and fifty-six miles in extent—is one of its most interesting features. They regard it as the most intricate and the most highly developed in the Mediterranean world. But to one of the rulers of prehistoric Knossos whom the ancients knew as Minos, the coastline was far from interesting. It was a troublesome problem and to solve it he finally had to accept the aid of Daedalus, an Athenian architect and inventor.

And so Daedalus built him the bronze giant, Talos, the first robot in history, to patrol the island three times a day, fire spouting from his mouth. For a long time the town of Phaestus, which lies southwest of Knossos, preserved the myth of Talos, somewhat idealized: a silver coin, struck in the fourth century B.C., shows the guardian of Crete as a youthful winged figure striding rapidly along and hurling stones as he goes.

Egyptian records know nothing of this mechanical man, but they have kept the name by which they knew the people. They called them *Keftiu* and carved them on their monuments, a slender-waisted, agile folk with dark, flashing eyes and proud bearing, ready to step forth and conquer the world about them.

Some scholars think that the name *Keftiu* should not be limited to the ancient inhabitants of Crete. It had a broader meaning, they hold, and embraced all the peoples who lived in the isles of the midland sea. Although Homer did not know of the name *Keftiu*, or at least did not mention it in his poems, he knew of the island and its people. Fabulous tales of their cities had drifted to his ears. He had heard that there were a hundred cities on the island and that the greatest of them was Knossos, where Minos lived and reigned. He had heard that Minos was reputed to be a son of Zeus, the mighty god, father of gods and men. Many more things he had heard, too, of Crete in the days of her ancient glory.

Until the latter part of the nineteenth century scholars knew little of prehistoric Crete except through its legends, various finds of gems, and sundry references in classical Greek literature. Greek literature presented a picture of a strong sea empire, a thalassocracy built on trade, in which people lived a civilized and orderly life. But the people who lived this pleasant life were all without faces, ghosts from the past who wandered aimlessly in and out of musty text-books and in and out of memories as well.

Today all that is changed. The fascinating science of arch-aeology has put faces on the *Keftiu*. Their existence un-dreamed of even by those who had lived all their lives in Crete, portraits of the *Keftiu* and their ancient palaces of stone had slept for many a century beneath the island's red poppies, her green olive groves, and her bright anemones. As evidence of a long-buried civilization began to appear under the spades of the archaeologists, the world learned that peo-ple had been living in Crete many thousands of years before the Christian era, perhaps even eight thousand.

The mound, *kephala*, or tell, into which Evans sank his first test pits, was not far distant from the site of the town called Candia when the island belonged to the Venetians but re-named Heracleion some time after it was officially in-corporated into Greece, in 1913. It was part of the good fortune which attended Evans that the huge mound proved almost at once to be the site of Knossos. Later on, when other archaeologists came to work in Crete, the excavations spread over the island with results that continued to surprise the world.

At Knossos the Palace of Minos was a revelation to every-one. Its foundations covered some six and a half acres, a con-fusion of endless corridors, halls, and rooms. At every turn might have been lurking the fabled Man-bull—or Bull-man, for what the ancients thought the creature to be is still hid-den in the mists of time; legend connected him with Minos and called him the Minotaur or Minos-bull, who fed on hu-man flesh.

In this palace where Minos lived and perhaps kept a mon-strous bull, life was luxurious. Here all the activities of the island had their focus; here a material level was reached that neither Egypt nor Greece ever attained. Established on a maritime basis, with an extensive and growing commerce, the Golden Age of prehistoric Crete equaled and in many ways surpassed that of Athens itself over a thousand years later.

So incredible were the rumors that spread through the ancient Greek world of life on the island of Crete that the legend of Atlantis arose, a legend that still pricks the imagination. Is Crete really the lost island of Atlantis, whose lofty mountains were clothed with green, whose rivers were alive with fish, and where game was to be had in plenty?

Plato calls Atlantis an island kingdom lying in the western ocean beyond the Pillars of Heracles. He describes it as an ideal commonwealth ruled by a powerful king who extended his sway over the neighboring islands and even made his way toward more distant parts of the world. Its busy harbor was filled with shipping; its merchants plied the seas; its wonderful palace was luxurious beyond imagining. He dwells at length upon the manner in which a bull is slain and its blood sprinkled on the pillar inscribed with the laws of the city.

Medieval writers who knew their Plato through Arabic sources regarded Atlantis as an authentic island, although they could not agree upon its location. Renaissance writers identified it with various places, including America. Today the submerged continent that, long before Plato's day, may have connected the eastern coast of America with the western coast of Europe, is thought by some geologists to have been the lost Atlantis. This takes us far from Crete. And the legend which makes Poseidon responsible for earthquake and flood that sank Atlantis deep into the western ocean cannot bring us back. Yet the aptness of Plato's description of the lost island still tempts the imagination. One still asks the question hopefully: Is Crete the lost Atlantis?

That question must doubtless remain forever unanswered.

But the magnitude of Cretan achievement suggested by other early references has been borne out by later discoveries.

Diodorus Siculus, the Greek historian who lived in the first century B.C., notes that in the opinion of many people the chief Greek gods came from Crete, and in this opinion some scholars of today agree. Cretan artists are said to have established schools of art in Greece itself, to which ambitious young artists came to receive instruction. The excavations have shown that Cretan architects surpassed in ingenuity and in practical skill most of their later followers in the ancient world. And that the island of the *Keftiu* early became a post of exchange in the Mediterranean is now well known. Little by little, Minos built up a formidable fleet of ships that became a familiar sight in many a harbor of the Great Green Sea. This maritime activity caused Crete to prosper mightily. Her unusual situation, at the crossroads of the sea lanes that led to three continents, did much to help her become the seat of the first thalassocracy in the history of western culture.

Those sturdy boats in which the early Cretan traders sailed were made of cypress wood and of cedar, with tall masts and high prows from which a fish or sometimes a fish pennant hung. Each had an oar which served as a rudder; with a good following wind they could easily have outrun their pursuers.

Though no one knows how much truth lies in the ancient accounts of the prehistoric fleets that are reported to have swept the Mediterranean free of pirates, dredging operations have brought up enough relics to lend some support to them. That the *Keftiu* were daring mariners and prosperous traders is certain. The story of the rise to power of the *Keftiu* and their fall is the story of the rise and fall of Knossos itself, whose rulers lived, generation after generation, in what was once the most extraordinary palace in history, the famous House of the Double Axe.

CHAPTER TWO

KNOSSOS IN THE DAYS
OF LEGEND

Among the tales still current in the Mediterranean, one
springs from a legend imprinted on an old Cretan seal-stone
which graphically illustrates the perils of the sea. Many an
old vase and seal-stone represent the fish-tailed Cretan ships.
This particular seal may symbolize the dangers they encountered as they played their parts in the building of a maritime
empire. It shows a grim-eyed, dog-headed monster climbing
up the steep sides of a small boat, while a rower with a long
pole tries desperately to drive the creature away.

Ancient tradition had known the sea monster as a maiden,
Scylla, who fell in love with Minos, betrayed her city to him,
and then tried to follow him home. In the act of climbing
aboard his vessel the gods had changed her into a monster.
Today she is a beautiful sea spirit, a *lamia*, who on moon-
light nights often clings to a passing caïque, crying out for
news of her lost son, Alexander the Great. If she receives the
wrong answer, she will destroy the caïque and all its crew.

Folklorists and anthropologists know that the number and

variety of traditions clustering about a place often help in judging both its importance and its antiquity. This is particularly true of Cretan legend, for although Homer speaks of numerous cities on the island, virtually all the legends that occur in both epic and classical literature are woven about Knossos, for centuries the most powerful city on the island.

The pleasant life at the court of King Alcinoüs, described in the *Odyssey,* may be a reflection of court life in Knossos; the freedom allowed the charming young princess, Nausicaä, may cast light upon the position of women at Knossos; Homer's mention of the special dancing place—or possibly the maze—which Daedalus built for the Cretan princess, Ariadne, casts added light. These stories of Nausicaä and Ariadne, and the brief account in the *Odyssey* of Minos as the friend and companion of Zeus, are only a few of the legends in Homer that point up the importance and antiquity of prehistoric Knossos.

The exploits of Minos are deeply embedded in many a legend of classical literature. One of the most familiar is associated with his conquest of Athens, which was long regarded as possibly true to history. Enraged by the murder of his son Androgeus, who had gone to Athens to attend games, Minos sought vengeance by attacking Megara, a strong ally of Athens, whose king was Nisos, the father of Scylla. After Megara had fallen into his hands through treachery, Minos sailed against Athens itself.

Each year after the fall of Athens, or each nine years—the legend varies—seven youths and seven maidens were chosen by lot and sent overseas to Knossos, there to be fed to the Man-bull. As the third time for the drawing of lots approached, Theseus, the son of the conquered king, Aegeus, volunteered to go as one of the victims, vowing that he would slay the monster and bring his companions home. Aegeus consented but begged his son, if he was successful—here one is

irresistibly reminded of the Tristram legend—to replace his
black sails with white ones.

In Knossos, Theseus met Ariadne, who promised to help
him if he would take her with him when he left Crete. She
then furnished him with a ball of wool and told him to fasten
the loose end to the entrance door of the labyrinth where the
Man-bull was imprisoned. He must then drop the ball on
the ground and follow it as it rolled mysteriously along in
front of him. Theseus observed his instructions, killed the
monster, retraced his steps by winding up the wool, and came
safely out.

Today visitors to the Candia Museum often pause before
a case in which a strange, hollow object about eight inches
long is cushioned. They see a unique clay vessel something
like an old-fashioned teapot, cylindrical in shape and provided with a loop handle. One end of the vessel is closed; the
other has a narrow slot-like opening just beneath a shelf-like
projection and just above two stubby feet on which the vessel
rests. In the body of the puzzling object are two small holes,
one on either side and opposite each other.

When it was found during the clearing of an earthquake-
stricken house in Knossos, someone suggested that perhaps
originally a rod had been inserted through the holes to act as
a spindle. A skein of wool, passed in over the shelf and
through the slot, might be twirled on the rod and emerge
through the slot as thread. Someone else suggested that perhaps the small vessel had once belonged to Ariadne herself.
Half in earnest, half in jest, the excavators christened their find
"Ariadne's Clew-box." And many a visitor has wondered
whether the Clew-box may not really have figured in the
old tale.

So popular was the story in antiquity that many versions
have survived. According to one, Minos was holding funeral
games when Theseus was brought in. Ariadne, who was present with the other women, fell in love when she saw him

throw his opponent three times. When she learned that the stranger was one of the captives newly arrived on the island, she determined to rescue him. Another version is that Theseus forced his way into the palace, met Ariadne, who had been left in charge during the absence of her father, concluded a treaty with her, and sailed away, taking her with him.

All versions agree that the bride never reached Athens, that Theseus left her behind on the island of Naxos when, forgetting to change his sails, he set out on his return trip. His father, watching for the ship, saw that her sails were still black. Unable to bear his anguish, he threw himself into the sea and was drowned. It was long a confirming tradition that the ship in which Theseus sailed was preserved in Athens as a sacred relic until about the third century B.C.

Until recently the legendary conquest of Athens by Knossos, with which the name of Theseus is associated, has withstood the test of time. Although investigation has shown that this supposition can no longer be seriously entertained, the ancient belief still persists that Minos once possessed a fleet of ships powerful enough to attack and overthrow Athens.

But prehistoric Knossos was superior even to fifth-century Athens in other ways, especially in its more sophisticated attitude toward women. This comes out clearly in the Ariadne legend. Her presence with the other women at the funeral games indicates that women could mingle freely with men; and that version of the story in which Theseus finds Ariadne in charge of the palace in her father's absence shows even more certainly the value placed on women in the Cretan code.

A few legends not essentially Cretan touch Crete at some point. Tradition includes the island, for example, among the various ports of call made by Jason, the leader of the Argonautic Expedition, as he was returning from the Black Sea with Medea and the Golden Fleece. At Crete, when he tried to land his ship, he was driven off by the bronze giant.

But Medea knew the secret of the robot's motive power: that throughout his body ran a single vein, and this ended in one of his heels. Instead of blood the vein contained a divine fluid, or *ichor*, identical with that in the veins of the gods. To keep the *ichor* in place Daedalus had closed the vein with a bronze nail. This nail Medea extracted, and soon the first mechanical man lay in ruins on the shore of Crete.

All legends are subject to interpretation, some logical, others apparently illogical. Ariadne has been variously interpreted not as a heroine of early romance, or as an early emancipated woman, but as a birth goddess, a moon goddess, and a goddess of vegetation whose annual disappearance came to be translated into terms of abduction. Later legend made Theseus her abductor.

One explanation offered for the myth of Talos derives from the belief that in prehistoric Crete the art of bronze casting may have been known. According to this explanation, the vein that ran through the giant's body represents the hollow center of the clay core and the nail the bronze pins that were inserted into the core.

Associated not so much with Knossos itself as with the whole general region of the island in which the ancient city was discovered, is the strange legend of the birth, death, and burial of the Cretan god Zeus, whom both Homer and classical Greek literature knew as the father of gods and men.

Legends of the birth and nurture of a divine child occur in many cultures. He is born under unusual circumstances, grows to manhood amid difficulties, and either dies a natural death and is replaced by another or is put to death by his enemies.

The parents of Zeus were Kronos and Rhea. Kronos had been in the habit of devouring his children as fast as Rhea bore them. He had already swallowed eleven by the time Zeus was born. Embittered by the loss of her other children, Rhea procured a stone, wrapped it up, and presented it to

Kronos, who promptly swallowed it. Metis, an obscure figure in mythology, forced him to disgorge the stone and with it the eleven infants he had previously swallowed. In this birth tale the stone Kronos swallowed represents, according to one view, the rude fetish form in which the Cretan Zeus, an indigenous god, was first worshiped. The primitive fetish belief of the early Mediterranean world slowly gave way to the new anthropomorphic belief that centered in the person of the Olympian Zeus.

The birth of a divine child was as easy for the ancient world to accept as it was for the apostle Paul. But to accept the Cretan assertion that Zeus was born on their island and had returned to die there was too repugnant for Paul. He branded the Cretans as liars. His feeling about the islanders might have been strengthened if he had known the tale still current in Crete, that outstretched on the rocky ridge of Mount Juktas lies the god Zeus, asleep forever on his mountain top. Today upon the summit may be seen the remains of an ancient sanctuary, still called by the countryside the tomb of Zeus.

The tale helps to emphasize the importance of Crete in the early history of the Mediterranean. Fantastic though it is, to see in it a symbol of the high and significant place which Crete was destined to achieve is not at all fantastic. For as she flung her empire farther out to sea, building ships with sides so steep that not even Scylla would have ventured to climb them, she was achieving Olympian heights in the empire building of the period.

CHAPTER THREE

THE BURIED CITY

One morning in 1878 a Cretan merchant whose name was Minos Kalokairinos (Minos Fairweather) was digging in his olive grove spread across the top of a large mound overlooked by Mount Juktas. Suddenly his spade struck something hard and rocklike. It proved to be part of a wall, built of enormous blocks of stone. Never had he seen their like. Digging deeper, he came upon what seemed to be part of the foundation of a building. It too was built of enormous blocks of stone. Then he uncovered large earthenware jars, some over five feet high, brightly painted and intricately patterned. Receptacles for oil, he thought, wondering why they had been buried in his olive grove.

Unaware that he was already digging a place for his name in the annals of Greek archaeology, Minos Kalokairinos continued to dig, hoping to find something of greater value than painted jars. When he had cleared away the earth to a depth of about seven feet, he saw openings in the wall, little more than holes, which seemed to lead into small rooms. Later he found blackened surfaces, apparently caused by fire. Strangest of all were peculiar marks or signs scratched here and there on the blocks of stone.

Although Minos Kalokairinos tried to keep his operations a secret, the news leaked out. It came to the ears of W. J. Stillman, an American correspondent for the London *Times*. Interested yet skeptical, Stillman arrived in Crete. Together the two men crawled through the openings in the wall into narrow passages, some only three feet high, and peered into cell-like rooms, choked with earth and fallen debris, in which they caught glimpses of painted interiors. The air was fetid, and they were soon glad to make their way out. Stillman then called his companion's attention to the way in which the wall angled and turned. Both men also examined again the signs scratched on the stone blocks but could still make nothing of them, except that one seemed to be the rough outline of a double-bladed axe.

The location of the find, the irregularity of the wall, the intricate passages, and the scratched signs led Stillman to conclude that the merchant had stumbled upon the labyrinth of legend, where the Minotaur had been imprisoned. The signs, Stillman thought, might be attempts at early writing, hieroglyphs perhaps, or perhaps they might even be clues by which the keeper of the Minotaur had made his way in and out of the labyrinth.

The stories Stillman subsequently wrote for the London *Times* attracted immediate attention to Crete. Jealousy caused the Turkish authorities—the island had belonged to Turkey for more than a century—to step in and forbid all further exploration of the site. Bitterly disappointed, Stillman left Crete. Today Minos Kalokairinos and W. J. Stillman have become mere names, thrust into musty archives and all but forgotten. Yet they deserve to be given their rightful place in history, for they were the first to point the way to prehistoric Crete.

Although the credit for discovering Knossos belongs prima-

rily to Sir Arthur Evans, who was knighted in 1911 because
of his find, he was not the first archaeologist to be attracted
to the site. The well-known German scholar, Heinrich Schliemann, read Stillman's accounts in the *Times* and hurried to
Crete. Behind him at that time were his excavations at His-
sarlik, which had roused both interest and skepticism when
he announced that he had found ancient Troy. Behind him,
too, were his discoveries at Mycenae, the reputed home of
Agamemnon, in which he had found in 1876 the deep shaft
graves, with their skeletons of men, women, and children, surrounded by priceless treasures in gold. And as a reward for
all this he had met less skepticism, for by this time it had
become increasingly obvious that Hellenic civilization had
existed centuries before the traditional date of the first Olym-
piad in 776 B.C.

Trusting to his own stubborn faith in Homer, Schliemann
pushed back thousands of years into the past the history of
Greece and wrote a new chapter in the annals of western
culture. But still to some extent he shared the skepticism of
his critics. And now with Stillman's accounts in his mind and
new hope he tried to get from the Turkish authorities the
permission to excavate which they had denied after Stillman's
revelations. The difficulties he met, however, proved insur-
mountable: in particular, the stipulation that anything he discovered would become the property of the Turkish government so discouraged him that he lost hope. This stipulation
is now made by all governments in countries where excavations are carried on, but in Schliemann's day it was unheard
of. It caused him to throw over the entire project and leave
the field clear for others.

Ten years after Schliemann's death in 1890, Evans re-
opened the effort. Undeterred by the stipulation that had
so disheartened Schliemann, he succeeded in buying from
the Turkish owner a quarter of the land he coveted. Then
he launched the excavations that were to result in the dis-

covery of the ancient civilization of Crete, for which the world owes him an incalculable debt.

Meanwhile, with a guide and pack mules Evans rode over the hills and through the valleys and glens of the island, becoming acquainted with the peasants, picking up engraved seal-stones, broken terra-cotta vases, fragments of relief work, peering with his nearsighted eyes into broken tombs, and gradually becoming convinced that, although nothing he saw reminded him of the historic Greece he knew so well, the original home of Aegean civilization would be found in Crete.

With the help of the funds he raised in England, and drawing freely upon his own private means—both Schliemann and Evans were wealthy men—he began in 1894 to conduct excavations in central and eastern Crete. He hoped to find out more about the strange signs Stillman had seen on the walls he and Minos Kalokairinos had uncovered. He found far more than the proof he sought, for, although his first campaign lasted just nine months, in this brief time he laid bare a hitherto unknown world.

In this undertaking on the island of Crete, a task which occupied him for the next thirty years or so and cost over a quarter of a million pounds, Evans had many colleagues. Without the help of Duncan Mackenzie, Theodore Fyfe, Piet de Jong, and many other associates he would have been severely handicapped. Mackenzie himself was an experienced archaeologist, Theodore Fyfe and Piet de Jong, professional architects. Mackenzie's successor, J. D. S. Pendlebury, was associated with Evans for five years. Later on, as the scholarly world became aware of what was happening in Crete, other nations besides England became interested, and archaeologists flocked from America, France, Italy, and Germany to the island to launch their own excavations. Prominent among them was a native archaeologist, Joseph Hatzidakis, at that time in charge of antiquities. All were richly rewarded, for they brought to light other long-buried cities, some of them with palaces almost as remarkable as the House of the Double Axe at Knossos. These cities provided additional proof of the high level of civilization that had been attained on the island.

Evans had come to Crete for the first time, in the spring of 1894, because he had seen peasant women in Athens wearing stones with strange marks on them. The women called them milk-stones, but neither they nor anyone else in Athens of whom he made inquiries could explain the meaning of the marks. The women said the stones were charms. Finally Evans discovered that the stones came from Crete. But when he reached Crete and tried to buy a milk-stone from a woman who was wearing one, she pointed to her baby, saying that he would die if she gave up her stone, because then she would have no milk for him. Later, as he began to find similar signs (rough crosses, serpents, windows) on various objects that he unearthed, incised not only on the blocks of stone where Stillman had seen them but on clay tablets, signet rings, and seal-stones, he realized that many were pictograms, an early form of writing with which Egyptologists had long been familiar, though no one had ever connected them with Europe.

When he next returned to England to raise more money he brought with him material proof that there had existed in Crete two kinds of writing: one "pictorial and hieroglyphic, the other linear and quasi-alphabetical," as the two systems were to be later described. After a winter in England he came back to Crete, only to encounter unexpected obstacles, including an uprising against further Turkish control of the island.

The uprising ended in 1899. The following year, when Prince George of Greece was appointed commissioner, Evans was enabled to begin digging in earnest. The results were startling. Great buildings came to light, a drainage system

constructed on scientific lines, gaily decorated stone bathtubs, beautiful frescoes, and exquisite jewelry, all proofs of
an advanced civilization surpassing anything ever found before in the Aegean world. The clue to the mysterious writing
still escaped detection, but the original home of pre-Hellenic
civilization seemed at last to have been found.

Would Evans have been greatly disappointed, one wonders, had he lived to hear that new excavations on the mainland of Greece have shown that the original home of European
civilization is now thought to be not in Crete but in Greece
itself, for in 1952, Professor George E. Mylonas of Washington
University found at Mycenae another circle of royal graves
at least a generation older than those discovered there by
Schliemann. In 1953, Professor Carl W. Blegen of the University of Cincinnati began excavating the site of ancient
Pylos near the western coast of the Peloponnesus, a little to
the north of the Bay of Navarino. These recent excavations
carry the history of Greece as far back as Evans carried the
history of Crete.

In view of the success which Evans achieved, it is notable
that he had done no digging on a large scale before Knossos.
His primary interest had been in numismatics. While still a
schoolboy at Harrow he had collected flints and coins. Old
coins seem to have had a special fascination for him, perhaps,
as his half-sister Joan writes, because his nearsighted eyes
could distinguish so easily the fine craftsmanship of ancient
seals and coins. Later his antiquarian tastes led him east to
the Balkan States and eventually to Crete.

He started his excavation of the huge mound with a crew
of only thirty workmen, all from Crete, but he soon had to
increase the number to one hundred. Later he employed even
more men. Photographs taken at the time show the men in
baggy Turkish trousers, their heads protected against the
sun by closely wound turbans, and their necks, as usual in
Mediterranean lands, protected by flaps of cloth hanging

loosely down over their shoulders. Evans himself generally wore the dress of an Englishman attired for the country. He invariably carried a walking stick—Prodger, his family called it—because of his poor eyesight. His men were fond of him, but there were some who were afraid of his temper.

As the workmen dug slowly down into the mound—from the beginning it was slow, hard work—they were almost more frightened than surprised to discover the size of the ruined stone building that came to light. Evans knew what Minos Kalokairinos had found; still, nothing in Greek legend or in literature had prepared him for the intricate structure that gradually appeared. The building itself consisted of two great wings, set on either side of a central court approximately six hundred feet long and four hundred feet wide. Evans knew that, according to tradition, Daedalus and his son Icarus had built a palace for Minos and that tradition also said it was from this very court they had started out on their homemade wings when they were forced to flee from Knossos.

What he did not know was that underneath the palace lay the ruins of at least two others, almost as extensive. Nor did he know that when he reached the First Palace he would have cut down through the accumulation of six centuries, counting back from the close of the Late Minoan Age in 1400 B.C. The highly finished stone implements he had discovered in his trial test pits showed that Knossos, settled as early as the Neolithic Age, was no less than three thousand years older than the Great Pyramid in Egypt. He found no traces of a settlement earlier than the Neolithic.

The stone axes, knives, spindle whorls, and other implements or tools discovered in Knossos had been rubbed by hand to bring them to a high polish, indicating that, although the potter's wheel had not yet been invented, an advance in civilization had already been made. These tools, as well as arrowheads, primitive hooks, bone awls, and carbonized grain in pots showed that the islanders had lived a life comparable to that found in other Neolithic cultures. Their men hunted game in the forest and fished in the surrounding waters or the island streams; their women learned to spin and to weave and to cook their food in pots.

Year by year the archaeologists laid bare not only the palace at Knossos but the surrounding town as well. It was estimated that at one time the entire site must have covered about twenty-eight acres. The town must, then, have been between twenty-two and twenty-three acres in extent. It was not merely an appendage to an acropolis; it grew naturally from a small unwalled settlement to a city of many-storied houses built of sun-dried brick or dressed stone. Here people of wealth and comparative culture lived a comfortable, prosperous life.

In the immediate vicinity of the palace, where the bulk of the middle classes lived, the population was about twelve thousand. In the suburbs the houses were not only smaller but were huddled more closely together than were those of the more prosperous citizens. Since Minoan houses at this time were often from four to five stories high the suburban population probably numbered about seventy thousand, making a total of eighty thousand people who, at the peak of Minoan greatness, lived in the city of Knossos. Some scholars have placed the figure even higher, around one hundred thousand.

The whole city was laid out according to a well-defined plan. The streets ran north and south, bisected by narrow lanes that divided the houses into blocks. As in modern cities, the houses were connected by party walls. Such systematic city planning would lend itself to indefinite expansion.

In general, these prehistoric houses resembled those still to be seen in Crete and in other Greek islands, where flat roofs, terraces, and outside stairways are common architectural features. The Town-mosaic, a series of glazed clay panels set into the sides of a wooden chest and representing Minoan house-fronts in miniature, shows houses of two or more stories, with windows of from four to six panes, made of some sort of translucent material, oiled parchment imported from Egypt, perhaps. The occupants of these houses were not altogether dependent upon windows for light. Like their betters, the common folk built their houses around an inside court, a kind of patio, also a common architectural feature in most southern building. Here, in those distant days, the children of Knossos may have played their games, perhaps splashing themselves and others in water from a fountain.

The interiors of the houses were smoothly plastered and painted in bright colors. Floors were either pebbled or painted, red being a favorite color for both walls and floors. The better houses had murals and may have been further adorned with gay cushions, as everyone hopes who has ever sat on a stone bench.

One peculiar feature of these houses at Knossos remains to be noticed. Many of them were set flush with the street, leaving no space for sidewalks. The doors were of wood, sometimes with an overhead transom. These doors did not stand in the center of a house-front but were sometimes to the right, sometimes to the left. Apparently their architects were not interested in symmetry, or else the people for whom they built were too individualistic to enjoy such regularity. It is possible that each house owner was his own architect.

During the third millennium the inhabitants of the island had learned to manufacture bronze. From then on they made rapid strides in civilization. Since the use of iron as a metal was not discovered until the twelfth century B.C., the entire intervening period elsewhere in the world had been known to scholars as the Bronze Age. Evans had the happy inspiration to perpetuate the semi-mythical name of Minos by calling the Bronze Age in Crete the Minoan Age.

In 1901, at a meeting of the British Association in Glasgow, he introduced his Minoan Age to the world. At the same time he announced that, to make this vast new civilization more comprehensible, he would divide his Minoan Age into Early, Middle, and Late Minoan. For the Early Minoan Age he set as rough chronological limits 3000–2200 B.C.; for the Middle Minoan 2200–1580 B.C., and for the Late Minoan 1580–1400 B.C. He was enabled to set up this system for Crete by correlating the stratigraphic evidence of his test pits with the dates already set for Egyptian civilization. Scholars have not always agreed with this classification, and some have made minor alterations, but on the whole his system has proved acceptable.

Some scholars call the entire Late Minoan Age the New Era or the Golden Age of Crete. Others prefer to confine the Golden Age within the narrower limits of 1450 and 1400 B.C. All agree, however, that the upsurge of building activity, or the palace period, began in the Middle Minoan Age, reached its peak in the Late Minoan Age, flourished for little over half a century, and then fell a victim to disaster. The earthquake of 1400 B.C. was catastrophic. To earthquake succeeded attack from overseas upon a weakened Knossos. And the insecurity and misery following invasion and earthquake brought about the so-called "palace revolution" which disrupted the old order.

The desperation of the people of Knossos when the earthquake stirred beneath them was brought dramatically home by the discovery of two small houses near the palace. Huge blocks of stone had been hurled down upon them. One was entirely crushed. The other, which had apparently been deliberately filled with earth after the catastrophe, proved when it was cleared to contain a sealed room, also filled with earth. Lying on the floor were several tripod altars and a bull's head with its horns intact. The excavators had learned enough to feel sure that this had been a propitiatory sacrifice to the underworld, that the bull had been killed outside the house, its head brought in and placed upon the floor, and the room then filled with earth and sealed, they surmised, with a curse invoked upon anyone who should ever unseal it.

Discoveries are not made all at once. Day after day, year after year the archaeologist watches his men delve into the earth. Often he finds nothing of significance. Then comes a day when a precious piece—a fresco, a figurine, or a gold pendant—suddenly appears, and his patience is rewarded. So it must have been with Evans and his colleagues when they discovered that beneath the foundation of the Late Minoan building which Evans had named the Palace of Minos, there were more palaces—how many he did not know at first—all waiting to be freed from the accumulation of centuries.

CHAPTER FOUR

THE THREE PALACES

Before considering the history of the three palaces that Evans found built one on top of the other it might be helpful to mention the threefold function of a Minoan palace. At Knossos the palace of the Priest-King was more than a royal residence. It was not only the seat of feudal government but also the center of religious life. Church and state were indistinguishable. The double axe was the Priest-King's chief sign of authority. The distinguished Swedish scholar, Martin Nilsson, considers this sacred emblem one of the three most important features of prehistoric Minoan religion, the other two being a pair of horns and a pillar. The presence in some form of all three of these features in each palace discovered in the depths of the mound has afforded convincing proof of the religious character of the Priest-King's palace.

In Egypt as in Asia Minor the divine nature of kingship was fully recognized, though in Egypt authority was divided between the Pharaoh and the somewhat more important priest. But in Asia Minor, which throughout the Minoan Age was one of the influential centers of the Mediterranean world, the situation was more like that in Crete. For the priest-kings of Asia Minor drew their power from deity itself, made manifest in a mother goddess, attended by a young male who was sometimes thought of as her son, sometimes as her consort. And in Asia Minor there also existed the cult of the *labrys*, or double axe.

The immense building that Evans unearthed he assigned to the Late Minoan Age. This building, partially reconstructed, which visitors see today, was not the first palace to be built on the site of the Neolithic settlement, but the third and last. Although the manner of its reconstruction has been sharply criticized it is a very real monument both to Minoan architectural skill and to modern scientific methods of excavation. Nowhere on the whole extensive site has the blunder Schliemann made at Troy been committed. In his inexperience Schliemann drove a great trench through his chosen site, destroying beyond recall important sections of the seven cities he afterward discovered, one underneath the other. It is only just to remark that Schliemann did not make a similar mistake at Mycenae.

Evans was also inexperienced, but he was not quite so impetuous as Schliemann. Moreover, Evans had the experience of D. G. Hogarth, at that time Director of the British School at Athens, to aid him, as well as the assistance of other experts. As a result, wherever possible the foundations of the two earlier palaces on which the third stood were carefully unearthed, photographed, measured, and studied, a task that involved years of painstaking work.

Since it would prove far too confusing to begin with the Third Palace and try to follow the workmen as they dug their way downward through the centuries, watching for traces of a people long dead, it might be better to begin where they ended, with the remains of the First Palace, and then to work our way upward.

The First Palace at Knossos was erected about 2200 B.C.,

at the close of the Early Minoan Age, or at the beginning of the Middle Minoan Age. The situation was a remarkably advantageous one, as the later history of the palace was to show. Barely three miles from a natural harbor, blessed with a plentiful supply of water, and close to the edge of a virgin forest, Knossos seemed to have everything in its favor.

In its earliest form the palace was composed of several buildings connected by causeways. These separate buildings are generally spoken of as "blocks," or *insulae*. To make room for them the whole top of the hill on which the original Neolithic settlement had grown up was leveled off, doubtless at the orders of the Priest-King then in power. The bulldozer had not yet been invented; so the demolition of early houses had to be done by hand, a piece of luck for posterity, since the foundations of some of these houses have been found. The leveled space formed a large central court, its major axis running from north to south. This court gave access to the various parts of the palace. Such, in essence, was the First Palace in the ancient city of Knossos: a central court flanked by two wings, one to the west, the other to the east. Its chief entrance was from the north, through a sea gate.

At this period in the history of the royal residence its first underground drainage system was built. Modern man takes his sanitary arrangements for granted, but to Minoan man a flushing system must have been little short of miraculous. So excellent was this system of fitted terra-cotta pipes and carefully built underground channels that few changes were made during the following centuries. Not so surprising but more important for the development of Knossos was the building of a road to connect the trade route from the south with the palace itself. Over this route merchants and traders from Egypt and Libya came, bringing their wares in exchange for what Knossos had to offer.

The earliest settlement on the hill had not been fortified, but the First Palace was protected by massive walls. In addition, near the northern entrance and the sea gate a tower had been built, apparently for defense. The walls of the First Palace are like the cyclopean walls that encircled the settlement on Mount Juktas, where the Cretan Zeus lay buried.

A kind of architectural unity was achieved when the various parts of the First Palace were consolidated into a larger whole. To achieve this, more early houses were destroyed, this time to the west, thus enabling the building to be extended in that direction. Walls were pushed back and the court enlarged and paved. Here three deep pits were found, possibly rubbish pits, unless they point to earlier building, for they held quantities of broken pottery. If rubbish was not left lying about, but regular places arranged for its disposal, some light is thrown upon the sanitary methods of the day.

The Second Palace, which clearly belongs to the Middle Minoan Age, was a more or less rectangular structure of some six acres in extent, with the enlarged court in the center. The two most important entrances remained those to the north and to the south. The entrance to the north was still through the sea gate, that to the south through a propylaeum, or porch, part of which was covered over. A double doorway gave additional protection to the inhabitants. The west wing contained the royal treasury, the king's throne room, and nearby a deep, sunken bath, or lustral area. A stone stairway with a balustrade led down into the bath.

Several of these baths were found in each palace. They were generally located near an important entrance and seem to have been designed for some kind of purification ceremony. This interpretation was confirmed by the later discovery beneath the ground floor of two small crypts in which sacrifices had been performed. In each crypt stood a square stone pillar, incised with the sacred emblem of Knossos, the double axe.

As the excavation of the Middle Minoan palace proceeded

it was found that not only had this Second Palace been erected around an enlarged court but that a whole new section had been added on the east side. Judging by the arrangement of its interior and the kinds of objects that were found, this section must have been devoted to the domestic life of the Priest-King. To build so extensive an addition he had his engineers cut far into the eastern slope of the hill where earlier a succession of terraces had been built. Here the great east wing took shape, with its brightly frescoed and pillared reception halls and its suite of rooms for the Queen.

The Priest-King had by this time so increased his trade with the countries bordering on the Mediterranean that he needed additional storage space. He provided for this by sinking deep trenches under the west porch and under the east wing. The trenches were divided into compartments faced with stone. Into the compartments were lowered huge jars of oil, grain, and other foodstuffs. By the time the excavators discovered these storage jars their contents had already been removed. But that a large proportion of them had contained olive oil is shown by the traces of combustion that occurred when toward the close of the Middle Minoan Age earthquake and flames partially destroyed the Second Palace. Additional confirmation came from the strata immediately underlying the trenches, where traces of carbonization also appeared.

The Royal Pottery Stores, as the excavators named the large collection of jars in the east wing and in the region directly to the rear, where more enormous jars—the giant pithoi—were stored, proved to be an unexpected treasure trove. Here, perhaps more than anywhere else in the excavations, convincing evidence appeared of the high artistic level which the Minoans had already attained. Delicate eggshell cups, beautifully shaped vases with well-turned spouts and handles, bowls with painted and fluted decoration, apparently in imitation of metal work, and painted libation pitchers

The Priest-King Fresco; the Palace of Knossos; photograph by **Alison Frantz**.

The Grand Staircase; the Palace of Knossos; photograph by Alison Frantz.

Harvester Vase; Candia
Museum, Crete; photograph
by Alison Frantz.

Chieftain Vase; Candia
Museum, Crete; photograph
by Alison Frantz.

Fresco (restored), Throne Room; the Palace of Knossos; photograph by Alison Frantz.

Toreador Fresco; courtesy of Candia Museum, Crete.

Gold Pendant with Bees;
courtesy of Candia Museum,
Crete.

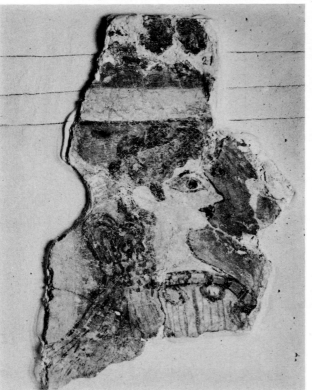

La Parisienne, Central Figure,
Ladies in Blue Fresco; courtesy
of Candia Museum, Crete.

Phaestus Disk; courtesy of Candia Museum, Crete.
(Approximate diameter: 6 inches.)

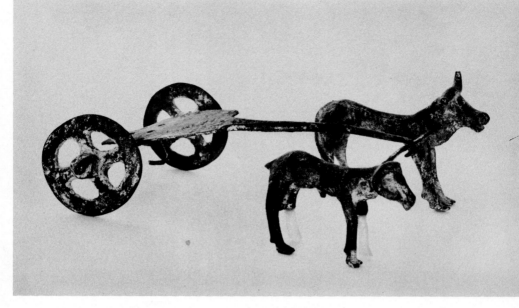

Miniature Cart; Candia Museum, Crete; photograph by Alison Frantz.

"Ariadne's Clew-Box"; Candia Museum, Crete; photograph by Alison Frantz.
(Approximate, length: 8 inches.)

made in the shape of a bull's head were among the many finds.

In a basement near the giant pithoi about four hundred pear-shaped loom weights were found. They are supposed to have fallen when the floor above was wrecked in the partial destruction of the palace. That the women's quarters were duplicated on the floor immediately above is inferred not only from the location of the loom weights but also from the discovery of a small terra-cotta shrine with sacrificial vessels that fell from an upper chamber. The chamber itself is thought to have been a sanctuary and to have been decorated with painted plaster dadoes, fragments of which were found above the loom weights.

Quantities of engraved seal-stones, made of rock crystal, liparite, and amethyst, were found, an indication that Minoan lapidaries were beginning to work in hard materials. One of the seals carries the impression of two heads: one of a man, the other of a young boy, possibly the actual portraits of a Minoan priest-king and his son. The seal itself may have been a royal signet, used by the personage whose portrait is engraved on it.

The catastrophe that almost completely destroyed the Second Palace occurred about 1700 B.C. The Priest-King who later rebuilt the palace did not have his workmen clear away all the ruins; he merely used the debris as filler and so gave unexpected aid to the excavators. While sifting through the debris near the place where the loom weights had appeared they found the remarkable Town-mosaic, which was most helpful in furthering the imaginative reconstruction of the city and which is now one of the treasures of the Candia Museum.

The third and last palace, built on the same site, was designed upon a grand scale. Perhaps the Priest-King now in power belonged to a new and more energetic dynasty. During this period, all too short in the cultural history of the

Mediterranean, Knossos reached so unparalleled a height of prosperity that it must have incurred the well-known jealousy of those gods who can not endure to see man draw too close to their own beatific state. Again nature intervened, and after a short but brilliant period she toppled man and his works once more into the dust.

The Priest-King who erected the Third Palace had no premonition of disaster, any more than his predecessors had had. His engineers seem to have proceeded as usual by removing all earlier debris and utilizing it as filler, with earth and stones added, especially on the east side, where the new domestic quarter had been built. To excavate this renovated quarter proved to be one of the most dangerous parts of the whole gigantic task. By great good luck two of the men had worked in the Greek mines at Laurion in Attica and understood how and when to insert props to keep their tunnels from caving in as they drove them, in mining fashion, deeper into the ruins of the earlier palaces.

One day the workmen, occupied on a paved surface they thought was the ground level, came unexpectedly upon a flight of stone steps leading upward. This was surprising enough, but soon they discovered another flight of steps at right angles to the first but leading downward. Real difficulties now arose. At each right-angled turn was a stone landing originally supported by wooden columns that were no longer in place. To keep the stone landings and the stairways from falling down on top of their heads as they removed the earth, the workmen had to insert wooden props at regular intervals. This was slow and risky work, for it took seven days to dig from the first landing down to the second. When the workmen finally reached the bottom of the long staircase they found themselves in a large colonnaded hallway that supplied light for five flights of stairs.

Visitors to Knossos may now descend this Grand Staircase, as it is called, all the way down to the colonnaded hall without running any risk of having rock piles crash down upon them, since cement columns have replaced the wooden props. But the clearing of the grand staircase was only the beginning. The workmen had to clear away the earth and debris that filled the ground floor of the enlarged domestic quarter of this Third Palace. Here, too, props were needed. The wooden beams that had originally supported an upper floor had long since disintegrated. This meant replacing the missing transverse beams by steel girders embedded in cement. While this work was being done an inner private staircase appeared. It was flanked on one side by the Queen's apartments and on the other by the Hall of the Double Axes.

This hall, named because the sign of the double axe was found on many of its stone blocks, was duplicated on the floor above, its location there being deduced from the bases of columns, so placed that they could only have been used to support an upper floor. Against one of the walls of the lower hall were found the remains of a wooden throne that had been covered with gold leaf, indicating that the hall might have served for state receptions. Easily reached by the grand staircase, its situation for such a purpose was admirable.

In addition to rebuilding the domestic quarter on a more magnificent scale than before, the Priest-King improved the various entrances to his palace. The sea gate now consisted of an inner gate and an outer gate, the two being connected by a covered passageway. Flanking towers and guardrooms were also built to render the palace secure against attack. A deep stone bath about seven feet square was built near this northern entrance. Here the Priest-King's visitors could perform the necessary rites of purification before they were admitted to his presence.

The royal or official entrance to the Third Palace was from the west. From this an elaborately decorated corridor led to the south propylaeum and thence into the spacious central court with its stone altar, its columns on either side, painted in brilliant colors, and its terraces with parapets of curving horns.

In the Second Palace the whole front of the west wing had been occupied by a set of storage chambers. To keep his growing wealth safe the builder of the Third Palace devised a new system. Instead of trenches he had deep pits dug under the floor of part of the west wing and his earthen jars put down into them. Innumerable signs of the double axe guarded this section of the wing.

Two years after the excavators had found the deep pits in the floor of the west wing, they made an even more important discovery. Noticing that the floor had sagged in one place, they had some slabs raised. Underneath were two large stone vaults. It was obvious that at some remote period robbers had broken into them and removed most of their contents; two battered stone hammers gave evidence of their presence, but they had not taken everything. What remained included a statuette of the snake-goddess, about nine inches high; terra-cotta offerings in the shape of robes, girdles, flowers, fruit, animals, and sea shells; and several small chalices, made of fine-glazed clay, from which libations may have been poured to the snake-goddess.

A shrine sacred to the goddess was also discovered in the Third Palace. Nearby, clay vessels were found, receptacles, perhaps, for oil for ritual purposes. In a small room stood several bird-shaped vessels, also of clay, that were associated with another religious cult, known today as the Cult of the Dove-goddess. Small replicas of double axes and of horns were also found.

In the Late Minoan Age the House of the Double Axe at Knossos reached its most magnificent stage. Its Priest-King was wealthy, and he seems to have lived upon a truly regal scale. His position as the head of a federation composed of most, if not all, of the cities on the island was now firmly established.

Relations with Egypt were happier than ever before. Knossos had staged a brilliant recovery from the catastrophes that had overthrown the two earlier palaces and had set out on a path of greater expansion overseas. At home her architecture, although it admitted innovations, had become more symmetrical, her system of writing had changed, her fresco painting was more finely executed, and her sculpture in the round more lifelike. Then in 1400 B.C. without any warning another catastrophe came upon her.

The earliest recorded earthquake occurred in A.D. 66 in the time of the Roman Emperor Nero. Since then a succession of shocks has been felt over a wide area, from Malta and southern Italy to the island of Rhodes. Lower Egypt, Alexandria, and Cairo have also felt shocks. Within the last few years disturbances have occurred in the Ionian Islands, in Northern Greece, and in the island of Santorin. In Crete, from the thirteenth century A.D. to the twentieth, thirty shocks have been recorded. At the time of the great earthquake of A.D. 1508 priests carried round the stricken city of Candia sacred images and even the Host itself, in a vain effort to stop the quaking of the island.

Evans, who experienced the earthquake of 1926, reports that the sound resembled the "roar of an angry bull." With such a fearful sound echoing in his ears he found it easy to believe that the Minoans might well have thought they had incurred the anger of an enormous beast, who, though he lived far beneath the ground, could bring their houses tumbling about their ears. And tradition may have handed down to them the terrifying knowledge, passed on from father to son, that in times past even the Priest-King's palace, protected though it had been by the holy double axe, had not always been immune.

CHAPTER FIVE

MINOS, PRIEST-KING OF KNOSSOS

The character, personality, and even the very existence of the powerful Priest-King who lived in the Third Palace are still matters of controversy. For no one knows whether his name was really Minos or whether Minos was the name of a dynasty, like that of the Pharaohs of Egypt.

One tradition states that there were two ancient kings by the name of Minos and that the one was the grandfather of the other. The genealogy involved in this tradition is generally discredited on grounds of improbability. Achaean legend mentions only one. According to the *Iliad*, this Minos lived in the second generation before the Trojan War, which ended when Troy capitulated in the twelfth century B.C. His daughter was Ariadne; his son Deucalion, the Greek Noah; his grandson was Idomeneus, who led a Cretan contingent to the assistance of beleaguered Troy.

The name Minos, whether it is that of a single individual or whether it belongs to a dynasty, has always been believed to have no connection with the Greek language. The same holds true of the names Knossos and Talos. Names ending in the suffix *os* are said to be characteristic of the Carian inhabitants of ancient Anatolia, where the ruling chief was also the spiritual head of his people, a priest-king. The title has long been associated with a well-known stratum of early religion, in which a king holds secular power only by virtue of his close relationship with deity.

Some authorities believe that the name Minos was borne by a succession of priest-kings, comparable to the Pharaohs. They base this belief upon the interpretation of archaeological evidence that points to an unusual degree of cultural continuity on the island, unbroken even by earthquakes. This unbroken continuity helps to justify Evans in his choice of the generalized term "Minoan" for the cultural and historical story of ancient Crete. He considers it far preferable—and in this most scholars agree with him—to the term "Knossian," which he characterizes as "too local and restricted."

It seems fair to assume, therefore, that at some period previous to the fall of Troy an individual by the name of Minos lived in Knossos and that he functioned as a priest-king. Both he and his predecessors, who may have borne the same name, lived on the site of the House of the Double Axe. Throughout its history his House was not only the residence of kings but also the center of religious life, the sanctuary.

In that early religious stratum from which the notion of a priest-king is derived, the relationship of a ruler with deity was not that of father and son, but rather that of mother and son. The chief deity in prehistoric Crete, as in Anatolia, was not male but female. In Crete she was a mother goddess, the source of all things that have life. Her representative on earth was the priest-king or, as some think, her son, born to her without male assistance.

In Homer, Minos is the son of Zeus and a mortal maiden, whose name, Europa, has little more than geographical significance. In the shape of a white bull, a favorite disguise

55

of the amorous god, Zeus had appeared before the daughter of King Antenor of Tyre, who, with her handmaidens, had come that day to the seashore. When Europa seated herself upon the bull's back he rose up, plunged into the sea, and swam away. In Crete he shed his bovine form and revealed himself to Europa in the glory of his godhead. From their union three sons were born: Minos, who became the king of Knossos; Rhadamanthys; and a third son, whose name is given as either Sarpedon or Aeacus.

Tradition is well within its rights in claiming divine descent for Minos. To trace the descent of a notable personage back to deity and by this means to enhance his prestige is a characteristic folk device. Ancient Egypt, for example, claimed divine origin for the Pharaohs; and Japan until quite recently thought of the sun as the progenitor of her royal family. To emphasize the paternal descent of Minos and ignore his maternal origin fits into the new pattern that was set in many early cultures when the facts of paternity came to be understood.

If Crete passed through the matriarchal stage, as some scholars think, perhaps no other explanation is needed. If not, then some ecclesiastical sleight of hand must have been required to establish the father-son concept upon a firm basis, since in prehistoric Crete church and state were one. And indeed today, though not of course completely one, they are inseparable, for every Greek child is born into his church as he is born into his country. Today, too, after the passage of so many centuries, the early concept of a holy Mother and divine Child still lives, and in a wider world than the world of Greece.

The *Odyssey* knows Minos as a child king and relates that he began his reign at Knossos when he was only nine years old. Although the passage in which this assertion occurs may not be wholly trustworthy it is possible that a youthful king once sat in childish majesty upon the ancient throne of Knossos.

But an altogether different legend relates that Minos had had some difficulty in trying to wrest the control of Knossos from the hands of its former ruler and that he had called upon Poseidon, the god of waters and of earthquakes, to assist him. Poseidon sent up a white bull from the depths of the sea, expecting Minos to offer it in sacrifice to him. Instead the new claimant to the throne, beguiled by the animal's beauty, added the bull to his own herd. In revenge Poseidon caused Pasiphaë, the wife of Minos, to conceive an unnatural passion for the bull. From their union the Minotaur sprang. In Minoan art the Minotaur is often pictured as an infant with a human body and a bull's head, seated upon the lap of his mother.

At certain intervals during his life Minos was obliged to ascend Mount Juktas to render account to his divine father. His strength replenished and his right to rule newly confirmed, he returned to his people. Tradition adds that during the period of the Priest-King's absence the whole island waited in fear and hope for his return, since no man knew whether his rendering of his account would prove acceptable or not. To avert possible disaster daily sacrifices were held. It has been suggested that the seven youths and the seven maidens who were sent upon regular occasions from Athens may have been sacrificed at this time as surety for the safe return of the Priest-King.

This tale of the close association of Minos with his divine father recalls a similar tradition about the Hebrew Moses and the Babylonian Hammurabi, each of whom is said to have received the law from the hands of deity. The Cretan tradition may point to the existence in Minoan days of an actual code of laws for which some ancient priest-king of Crete may have been responsible.

In the Babylonian law, which was almost contemporary,

the position of a woman was relatively high; she had the right to own and to dispose of property and even to divorce her husband if sufficient grounds could be proved. It would be striking, indeed, if some day when the Minoan documents are fully deciphered history could record that the Minoan woman occupied as high a position as that of her Babylonian sister.

Later Greek tradition made Minos himself into a lawgiver, a tradition which is supported, in part, by the clay documents that were unearthed at Knossos. Ancient historians say also that Minos was the first to build up a navy and that with his ships he gained control over the Cyclades and warred against the pirates who infested the eastern Mediterranean. Recent investigation has established him further as the head of a federation of cities on the island. He is also said to have led a force against Sicily and to have founded in the western part of that island a town, later known as Minoa. The name occurs here and there in the Mediterranean area. It seems to have been used to indicate the presence of various colonies sent out by prehistoric Knossos and is considered additional proof that a personage by the name of Minos did indeed exist in the island of Crete. In Sicily, so it was said, Minos was killed, apparently by treachery, and a tomb erected over him. Discovery of a town on the ancient site of Minoa helps to confirm this old tale of a Sicilian expedition.

Diodorus Siculus has left a rather gruesome account of the death of Minos. When he arrived in Sicily he took refuge with a certain king, Kokalos by name, who killed his guest by pushing him into a tub filled with boiling water. Could the story have sprung from the sight of those Minoan bathtubs that differ little in appearance from coffins, and that seem to have served, at times, a double purpose? Legend adds the finishing touch to the life of Minos. For his administration of justice while on earth, and for his other good deeds, he became a judge in the After World.

Scholars who have pieced together all the various traditions associated with the name of Minos have discovered what almost amounts to a split personality. He is cruel, tyrannical, and destructive; he is generous, kindly, and constructive. He had a dungeon under his palace, into which he threw his captives, alive, to be torn in pieces and devoured by his Man-bull. He was a "patron of the arts, founder of palaces, establisher of civilized dominion." If the same critical method were to be applied to the Pharaohs a similar difficulty would arise. There were many Pharaohs: some were cruel and vindictive; others were wise and kind. The Minos of the split personality seems then to give evidence that the name represents not merely one ruler but a dynasty. Yet in the absence of definite records from Crete the reader is at liberty to give free rein to his imagination and either build up a composite Minos who functioned as a priest-king or, better still, follow the example of the historic Greeks and admit that he has little or no interest in questions of origin. It was enough for the Greeks that in Knossos in the days of her glory there was a powerful ruler whom they knew by the name of Minos, whom they once had had occasion to fear, but who was now safely dead and buried.

Like the *Keftiu,* his people, this powerful Priest-King of legend and early history had no face, no lineaments, no visible person. But slowly, as the excavations proceeded, he or his dynasty took on visible form.

The aquiline features of the two portrait heads, one of a man and the other of a young boy, which may well be those of a Minoan priest-king and his son, are repeated in a painted relief found almost intact on a wall of one of the corridors of the Third Palace. This depicts a man of commanding presence upon whose brow rests a plumed crown made of lilies, the sacred flower of Crete. A lily collar adorns his neck. He walks in a field of lilies, leading his sacred beast, a winged creature, his holy griffin.

The Chieftain vase, a goblet made of steatite, or soapstone, and found at Hagia Triada in southern Crete, shows an equally majestic figure. He wears a striped loincloth, a long triple necklace, and high boots. Except for the necklace his chest is bare. In his right hand he holds a great staff firmly planted on the ground and fully as tall as he. Before him stands a smaller figure with a file of soldiers at his back, a lieutenant, perhaps, to whom the Priest-King is issuing orders.

The Priest-King is often pictured with various animals: a lion, a wolf, or a wild cat. Occasionally an owl or a dove appears, or a dolphin, perhaps to signify his control of the sea. The seated cat that appears on one of the faces of a fine red cornelian seal and that may have been his personal badge suggests a close association between Crete and Egypt.

Whether portrayed alone or with one of his animals or holding in his hand a spear or a double axe, the Priest-King is an aristocrat, born to command. Both judge and jury, from his decision there was no appeal. With an absolute power based upon force and upon religion he made the laws and through his subordinates compelled observance of them. He had an elaborate system of signing and countersigning, scores of official seals, and a well-organized government. Under his rule Knossos attained a position that must have excited the envy of all her neighbors. Foremost in the export-import trade and in full mastery of the sea lanes, both Minos and his people prospered and were as content as the Earth-shaker would allow them to be.

Minos had his signet ring, and with it he sealed his coffers that all might know his mark and accord it the respect that was its due. This signet ring, the "very emblem of Minoan civilization," may be identical with one found at Knossos, for near the Kairatos River a gold signet ring was picked up, not far from a tomb that had already been plundered before the excavators unearthed it. Since the tomb had obviously been intended for a person of rank it is thought that both ring and tomb must have belonged to a priest-king, a Minos of Crete.

During the greater part of the year Minos lived in his palace at Knossos with its open courts, its royal hall and audience chamber for the king, and its separate quarters for his queen. About the beginning of the Late Minoan Age a smaller palace was built, connected with the larger residence by a kind of *Via Sacra*. Although this smaller establishment may have served as a summer residence, its primary purpose was religious. Apparently built directly after the great earthquake of 1570 B.C., the Little Palace may have been intended as a propitiatory offering to the underworld powers. This interpretation of the building is borne out by the discovery that about a quarter of its total area consists of underground chambers, in which massive pillars had been erected. In these chambers, or pillar crypts, worship, perhaps consisting largely of the sacrifice of animals, was paid to the dreaded gods of the underworld. As in all buildings in Minoan Crete devoted either in whole or in part to religious purposes, a lustral area was set apart for ritual cleansing. The lustral area here was unusually large in proportion to the small size of the palace; additional evidence that the whole palace was intended as a propitiatory offering.

The Little Palace, when excavated, told its own story of attempts at appeasement. Its pillar crypts were filled with offerings. Among them was a magnificent libation pitcher of black steatite made in the shape of a bull's head. Its wide, curving horns still showed traces of their gold plating. In one crypt a stand for a double axe was found, and nearby a rude but unmistakable image of the snake-goddess. Into this sanctuary many a priest-king may have gone to perform ceremonies which he hoped might avert fresh catastrophe. Perhaps he assisted at the sacrifice of a bull and watched anxiously until his attendants, using the pitcher with the gilded horns, had caught a supply of warm blood to carry into a crypt and pour on the ground at the foot of a pillar. For an ancient priest-king of Crete, whether his name was Minos or not, had many responsibilities and duties, combining in his own person, as he did, the double function of ruler of the state and spiritual head of his people.

CHAPTER SIX

THE FRESCOES

The task of excavating the Third Palace was proceeding
methodically, each day bringing to light new finds that kept
everyone alert but only mildly excited. Then during the first
week of April a series of more truly exciting discoveries began
to be made. The workmen were engaged in clearing a narrow
corridor in the west wing, near the south propylaeum. As
they carefully removed the layers of earth they came upon
fragments of painted stucco lying on the rubble-encrusted
floor. From one of the fragments a human face stared up at
them.

The workmen thought they had found a sacred icon. They
crossed themselves and waited for instructions. Further
search revealed more fragments; imagine the surprise of the
excavators when they realized that the fragments were part
of a fresco and the pigments had been applied to the surface
of the wall while the stucco was still moist. What they were
looking at was true fresco painting of a high order.

It would have been too much to expect that a mural
painted thousands of years ago could have been preserved

intact. This time fortune had been kind, for the greater part
of the fresco was in two large pieces. But each had suffered
some damage, and to remove them without causing irrepara-
ble injury was a delicate task involving the insertion of fresh
plaster under the pieces. When this was done and the parts
fitted together, enough of the fresco remained to show a
finely executed male figure, a young Minoan, the first ever
to be seen by modern eyes. He was clad in a short loincloth,
striped in red and blue and richly embroidered. On his
shoulder he carried a tall, cone-shaped vessel. That the
original had been made of gold and silver seemed indicated
by its yellow and blue paint. The same yellow and blue
showed ornaments of gold and silver adorning his person,
possibly indicating his rank.

To Evans and his associates the appearance of so finished
a mural was amazing enough, but to the Cretan workmen
the emergence from the heaps of rubble of a human figure
colored as brightly as though it had been painted only the
day before was nothing short of a miracle. They were quite
willing to stand guard over their find as long as it should
be necessary. Indeed, Manolis, the foreman, watched over it
all night and in the morning told Evans that he had seen
lights play about it in the darkness.

The figure was considerably taller than the average Minoan
of his day, as was learned afterward by comparison with parts
of skeletons well enough preserved to be measured. The
mural, or Procession Fresco, of which the Cup-bearer, as he
is now called, formed a part, showed a procession of men and
women advancing in single file toward the palace, some forty-
eight in number and each as tall as the Cup-bearer. In
addition, the mural is estimated to have contained over five
hundred smaller figures, an impressive spectacle to a visitor
entering by the south porch.

The procession, some think, may have commemorated a
religious ceremonial in which the sacred vessels were carried

out to be shown to the people. Others think that the artist may be representing a mission to the Egyptian Pharaoh, before whom the Minoans came to lay their treasures, not as inferiors but conscious of their own proud inheritance as members of an equally powerful nation.

Today replicas of the Cup-bearer appear in all archaeological collections. When he was photographed and published and the world had a chance to share vicariously in his discovery, interest in the excavations rose perceptibly. At last people could gain some visual image of these islanders who lived so long ago in the midst of the Great Green Sea.

The Cup-bearer's features are not Semitic. His dark, slightly almond eyes, black curling hair, and short compact frame make him easily recognizable as a member of the European race. The bridge of his nose is fairly straight; the nose itself, finely cut and tilted slightly upward. The reddish color of the flesh is familiar to Egyptologists as a characteristic of male portraiture. The pigment is identical with that formerly used in Egypt and may have been an Egyptian product.

The entire mural had been executed in pure lime plaster, a process that experts have now traced back to the Neolithic Age. Despite certain archaic touches, such as the eye drawn full front, although the torso is in profile, the mural has aroused general admiration and is recognized as being equal in execution to the early Italian fresco painting of the thirteenth century.

Except for silver anklets and silver armlets, a necklace and earrings, the Cup-bearer wears only a loincloth. But suspended from his left wrist hangs a seal, apparently made of agate; his "identity bracelet," it has been called. Many such seals have been found: some may have served as charms, others for stamping important documents. Upon his forehead the Cup-bearer has a strange bluish mark that has been interpreted as tattooing, but whether the mark means anything other than mere ornamentation no one has yet discovered. The Cup-bearer no longer looks out upon passing visitors from his original station in the mural; he now occupies a prominent place in the Candia Museum, while his replica stands in his former position in the south porch of the palace.

The Procession Fresco belongs to the time of the Third Palace, the Golden Age of Crete. During this period large wall spaces began to be fully appreciated for their decorative value. Although later in the excavations other extensive murals were found, the most impressive example remains the Procession Fresco, and the corridor in which the fragments were discovered is known today as the Corridor of the Procession. Unfortunately, of the entire fresco, with the exception of the Cup-bearer, only the reddish-brown feet of the men and the white feet of the women have been preserved, with the slightest indication of richly decorated clothing above.

The effect this great fresco must have produced upon the spectator is best seen in the imaginative restoration by Messieurs Gilliéron, father and son, and published in *The Palace of Minos*. Here the young men carry vessels of gold and silver; the young women, musical instruments: the sistrum, the pipe, and castanets. Both men and women are dressed in what seems to have been the fashion of the day: their heads bare, with long wavy hair falling down over the back; the young men in short kilts, richly embroidered; some of the young women in flounced skirts; others in plain ones reaching to embroidered hems.

Less than a week after the discovery of the fresco the Priest-King's audience chamber was found. A gypsum throne with a high, carved back stood against one wall. Stone benches, accommodating at least sixteen persons, extended along either side. The floor was littered with relics of past glory: lapis lazuli, fragments of gold foil, miniature crystal plaques, and other ornaments. Opposite the throne stone steps led to a sunken bath like that in the earlier palace, paved with stone slabs. Here the Priest-King's councilors may have cleansed themselves, or perhaps the Priest-King himself was anointed here before seating himself upon his royal throne— the oldest throne in Europe.

The chamber is richly frescoed. On the wall on either side of the throne two pairs of painted creatures—their original colors restored—face each other, dragons or griffins, Evans thinks, though they have no wings. They may have been thought of as companions or guardians of the Priest-King. They are elaborately decorated in green, red, and blue, and they transfix the spectator with their glassy stare. Elsewhere the chamber seems to have been frescoed with river scenes or with tall reeds or grasses in naturalistic designs.

In this ancient audience chamber, where Minos once sat and administered justice, no warlike scenes occur similar to those often found in Egyptian tombs, where the walls are painted with the exploits of long-vanished Pharaohs. No warriors in full panoply are here, nor wretched captives dragged along behind a victor's chariot. In the Minoan throne room the decoration was peaceful, as though the Priest-King may have retired to his chamber to seek repose of spirit.

As the clearing out of the Third Palace went on, painting after painting came to light: delicate olive sprays in full flower, plumaged birds, royal ladies in low-necked gowns and adorned with necklaces of precious stones, a young girl so exquisitely turned out that she was at once called *La Parisienne*, although it must be admitted that she has often been called a minx. On one red-letter day there appeared the spectacle of a charging bull, and then the Toreador Fresco, showing a young man and two girls, the young man in the act of somersaulting over the back of a galloping bull. One of the girls stood between the great pointed horns, and behind the beast stood the other girl, apparently waiting to receive the vaulter the instant his feet touched the ground.

The Toreador Fresco was found broken into innumerable

fragments near a small court of the palace. When the pieces were put together the fresco became the center of a prolonged controversy. Was it possible, scholars inquired of each other, for even a young and agile youth to grasp the horns of a bull at full gallop and swing himself onto its back? Would he not be gored to death before he could gain sufficient momentum to fling his body upward for the stance essential to a somersault? And what of the girl in front of the bull? Her position between the horns seemed to indicate that she was only waiting her turn to imitate the performance of the boy. Rodeo experts who were consulted pronounced the entire feat completely impossible.

Later discoveries, however, made it clear that, impossible though this particular exploit might seem to modern eyes, difficult and highly skilled bull-grappling stood high in the esteem of the Minoans. Bull sports were a favorite theme for frescoes and for painted stucco reliefs. And bull-grappling was not merely a sport; like other activities of ancient Minoan life, it was bound up with the worship of the Mother Goddess.

The fresco in which *La Parisienne* appears is one of a series of panels showing men and women seated on low stools, some holding goblets apparently made of precious metals. Although the painting belongs to a somewhat later period than that of the Cup-bearer, experts say that it still shows signs that the artist was not yet fully at home in his medium. Especially noticeable is the sketchy delineation of the ear and the rather careless rendering of the curls. But all agree that the young woman is alert, intelligent, and vivacious, an excellent representative of the old Mediterranean race.

La Parisienne wears a large butterfly bow attached to her shoulders. Scholars thought at first that the knot was a part of her costume. Later on, when they found similar knots painted or incised on various objects associated with Minoan religion, they began to think that *La Parisienne* wore a shoulder knot to show that she was devoted to the service of her Goddess.

From the number of women in the frescoes one must conclude not only that the painters of the day found the elaborate costumes of the ladies an absorbing theme but that there could have been few restrictions upon a woman's activity. In the brilliant days that mark the height of Minoan civilization, about the middle of the fifteenth century—some put it earlier—the frescoes show groups of seated ladies, elegantly dressed, engaged in animated conversation with each other; leaning out over their window sills; rubbing shoulders with the men at the public spectacles, to which every one seems to have been admitted; and generally enjoying themselves far more freely than was ever true even in the Golden Age of Greece.

Some of the Miniature Frescoes portray highborn ladies wearing strings of beads and brilliant jewels. In one of these frescoes the ladies are watching a sacred dance that is being performed in a grove, or a walled enclosure. To indicate the dense crowds of spectators, who are also watching the dance, the artist has employed what Evans calls "artistic shorthand," a technique comparable to that of modern line drawing.

This same technique occurs in the Temple Fresco. On either side of a small shrine and pillar are grandstands filled with gaily dressed ladies, and below them crowds of people, men and women, mill about. That the fresco had originally consisted of several panels was assumed from the large number of fragments. The technique in use is clearly discernible. Twisted threads, or something similar, Evans and others think, were inserted in the fresh plaster to mark the lines the painter intended to follow. A single sweep of his brush would then be sufficient to wash in his color. He could add the details later. It has been estimated that in the Temple Fresco some six hundred people were represented, and the larger Dance Fresco may have contained about fourteen hundred.

Although complete knowledge of Minoan fresco painting is still lacking, since no one knows how the lime plaster was actually produced, scholars have noted a definite artistic growth. They feel that the artist gradually attained a greater purity in line and a remarkable skill in working in two dimensions. They admire his ability to show people talking and gesturing excitedly. This is especially noticeable in the fresco, the Ladies in Blue, in which the subjects are obviously talking with one another. From this the conclusion has been drawn that the use of gestures to supplement the spoken word must have been fairly common. The gestures of these ladies are always restrained, however, another indication of the high level which Minoan civilization had reached.

The discovery of the Caravanserai, near the House of the Double Axe, and of another building, called the House of the Frescoes, has added greatly to the reputation of Minoan artists. Here the decorative possibilities of winged creatures, of flowering plants, and of vegetable life were widely explored. The House of the Frescoes centers its interest upon wildlife—the blue monkeys are especially admired—and upon scenes from nature: flowers of many kinds, particularly lilies and wild roses, irises and crocuses; clumps of other vegetation, too, and rocky landscapes and seascapes. Human activities seem to interest these painters far less than the varied life of nature.

These frescoes by no means exhaust the list. Many more, either in their original fragmentary condition or in excellent restorations, may be seen in museums. They come not only from Knossos but from many other places in Crete where excavations have been undertaken. For example, at Hagia Triada a finely executed fresco showing a wildcat stalking a pheasant was found in the palace. Wildcats appear fairly often in Minoan fresco painting. Sometimes they pursue wild fowl, ducks, or pheasantlike birds. In the Hagia Triada fresco Mrs. Harriet Boyd Hawes, an early associate of Evans, finds an emotional quality. She speaks of the "quiet confidence of the unsuspecting bird . . . and the cautious tread of the prowling cat."

The use of plaster for wall surfaces is supposed to have originated from the need to protect the loose rubble and sun-dried brick out of which walls were usually constructed. In the early days a single color, a red ocher, was used. It was applied indiscriminately to walls and pavements in much the same way as it is today in Cretan villages. Afterward more colors were added. A deep, natural blue was developed and still later a brilliant, cobalt blue, the pigment perhaps coming from Egypt.

Minoan use of this blue paint is best seen in the House of the Frescoes, where the blue monkeys appear. Fresh study of their color has caused a new appraisal to be made of the blue paint in the fresco from Hagia Triada long known as the Saffron- or Crocus-gatherer. Comparison of the two paints has finally almost settled the long-standing controversy over the interpretation of the Crocus-gatherer. Today it is thought highly probable that the figure is not that of a human being but of a blue monkey. Some think that a tail is distinctly visible. Surprisingly enough, if the figure is a monkey, he is putting crocuses into a bowl.

Minoan painters not only utilized their large wall spaces for frescoes in which hundreds of people were sketched in; they were also perfectionists in detail. In one fresco a small, frightened mouse crouches at the foot of a cluster of reeds. The tip of the little creature's tail curls about the slender spike of a reed, holding his body motionless in the face of danger.

CHAPTER SEVEN

THE UNDERGROUND
DRAINAGE SYSTEM

The Byzantine cisterns of Constantinople and the famous underground sewers of Paris have always roused admiration. But the surprise they excite in the mind of a world traveler is nothing, compared with Evans's astonishment when during the season of 1902 he discovered the first traces in Knossos of an underground drainage system.

Working without the benefit of modern laboratories, indeed with little or no mechanical aid of any kind, Minoan engineers contrived a sanitary system not only more elaborate and extensive than any other contemporary achievement but, though it seems primitive today, unequaled anywhere for many centuries to come. Bathrooms and flush toilets may not be as romantic as the young Cup-bearer who emerged from the depths of the earth; still, imagination and inventive skill went into their making just as into the frescoes.

For an island like Crete, which suffers violent extremes of weather, the problem of drainage is acute. Necessity mothered their invention—it must in hot countries—but surely imagination fathered it. For they were the first, specialists say, to develop the theory of the parabolic curve. Upon this, they constructed their runnels so that by a series of curves the flow of water could be checked wherever necessary. Some of their terra-cotta pipes for conducting the water to the main channel were straight; others were curved. All were carefully tapered at one end, equipped with collars and stop-ridges, then cemented together. Today sections of pipe over two feet long, tapering from six inches in diameter to four, can still be seen where they were originally laid.

The drainage system, begun when the First Palace was built and continued during later rebuilding, was so thoroughly laid out and constructed that few major changes, beyond extending the system to include the east wing, had to be made. Each block of the palace had its own separate system, connected, however, with one of the branches of the main channel.

After all these thousands of years the system at Knossos still works. Not long ago a party of sight-seers was being shown over the site. Their conductor was explaining the system in some detail when a hard rain began. To the surprise of everyone water came rushing down through a pipe near them.

Some of the drains that carried off the waste were so huge and so well ventilated that the workers on the excavations could walk through them without stooping. They could also remain in them whole days without discomfort. Obviously, in Minoan times these great drains could have been cleaned out whenever it became necessary. Stone conduits led the rain water from the roofs and the waste from the different floors of the palace into the main channel. Here all the separate branches met to discharge their waters into a nearby stream.

Along the various outer stairways of the palace, drains with convex curves to break the flow of water had been constructed. Without them the torrential rains, frequent at cer-

73

tain seasons, would soon have destroyed the best-built stairs. Visitors who are interested in the Minoan drainage system are always shown the east bastion of the palace, where a narrow channel, now restored, runs along the stairway leading down from the bastion. At each step there is a convex curve. When the channel reaches the lowest step, it turns sharply outward and deposits its burden in a settling-basin, where impurities are left before the water continues its course down the hillside. In Minoan days the rain water, diverted in this manner, may have been led into nearby washing tanks where the women would wash their clothes, amusing themselves by exchanging tidbits of gossip as they worked. They did not need to go to a river, like Nausicaä and her maidens.

Little is known of the way in which water was piped into the palace, but that it must have been brought in, at least for drinking purposes, has been conjectured from the discovery of small pipes of hard-baked clay. Many of these, tapered at one end and fitted one into the other, could have been used for bringing water from even distant springs. The excavations have shown that in Minoan days adequate springs existed fairly near the site of the palace, though over the centuries decreasing humidity has reduced their waters to a mere trickle.

That water for other purposes than drinking must have been piped in seems clear from the large number of bathrooms and latrines that were found in the palace. Although no tubs were actually found in place, many tubs, some whole, some in fragments, were discovered in corridors and rooms. Indeed, the number of bathtubs found on the site of Knossos and elsewhere on the island enables scholars to trace the change in shape that took place in them over the centuries. It is hard to decide whether these changes preceded or followed the changing fashion in coffins. As rectangular coffins began to displace the earlier round ones bathtubs fitted with lids seem to have come into use. Often the only distinction between a rectangular tub and a rectangular coffin lies in the painted decoration. This is particularly true when handles are attached to a tub. Perhaps such receptacles were actually used for a double purpose, a man's tub serving him as well in death as in life.

In the east, or domestic, wing of the palace several latrines were discovered, all in the Queen's suite. One was on the ground floor; the others, of which only a few traces remain, were on the floor above.

South House, the home of a well-to-do Minoan family, was equipped with a latrine built into one end of a narrow room which was lighted by a small window. The excreta were flushed down a vent into a covered pit with water brought in from the roof through a clay pipe.

No evidence has yet appeared that Minos and his family enjoyed the luxury of a hot-water system, but since there was some sort of arrangement for heating water at the royal guest-house, or Caravanserai, where travelers may have been accommodated, the King's family is likely to have been as well served.

The excavations conducted on the site of what proved to be the Caravanserai disclosed an elaborate sunken bath about five feet square, situated just off the courtyard into which travelers would come when they first arrived. The bath itself was deep enough to have reached to the knees of an average Minoan man. It had two entrances, one from the courtyard down a flight of three steps, the other from the guesthouse down a flight of five steps. Although foot washing seems to have been required before entering a house this particular bath could also have been used for a hip bath. Stone slabs, projecting out over the water, provided seats for the bathers. In one of the corner slabs a hole had been bored, through which water could escape when the bath had to be emptied.

The discovery of the bath and of the Caravanserai which

75

it served is too dramatic a story to be omitted. One day Evans noticed south of the palace a place where some unusually tall and unusually green barley was growing. Looking about for some reasonable cause, he saw that a small brook was flowing close by the stand of barley and that the brook was fed by a spring. He also observed that the spring was not far distant from the South Road, over which travelers had to pass on their way to the palace.

With that sixth sense all archaeologists seem to possess Evans decided he had probably come upon something important, and he began at once to make inquiries. Soon he learned that the Turkish bey who lived nearby had been digging about and had come upon some blocks of dressed stone. This was news. Evans immediately set about obtaining permission to excavate. When he obtained the permission he put his men to work.

Their reward came almost at once. Under the patch of barley they discovered a stone bath through which water was still running into a stone trough just the proper height for watering animals. As the excavation proceeded Evans realized that he had stumbled upon a unique building, which he afterward suggested might have served as a resthouse for travelers, especially those who came by way of the South Road. The newly arrived traveler, as weary and dusty from his journey as his ass or oxen, could cleanse himself in the bath, slake his thirst from the pipe which brought spring water to the trough, and eat his food in a room decorated with a frieze of partridges. At night he and his pack animals could sleep in the courtyard, or, if the incomplete evidence can be relied upon, he could sleep in an upper room, while his beasts were stabled in a basement with cobbled floor and bins for grain. The arrangements of this handsomely decorated building remind those who are familiar with accounts of even early nineteenth-century travel in the Middle East, of the large caravanserais there, in which men and beasts were accommodated.

That water might have been heated for the Priest-King's guests has been thought likely from the discovery in a small room of a waste duct to which carbonized particles were still clinging. Also, fragments were found in the room, which, when pieced together, turned into painted bathtubs. These finds indicated that Minos might have had a hot-water system of some sort in his guesthouse.

Soon a more interesting discovery was made. For near the Caravanserai the excavators laid bare an underground stone chamber that had been built over a spring. And in the debris which had choked this spring through the centuries they found decorated cups, incense burners, even bowls containing bits of food. When they had finished clearing the spring and had restored the flow of the water they realized that they had before them a deep foot bath similar to that of the Caravanserai. In one corner of the chamber near a niche hung a stone lamp, and just outside lay fragments of other stone lamps, intended, no doubt, to provide light for persons who came to fill their water pitchers.

The cups, incense burners, and bowls of food that appeared in the debris were interpreted as votive offerings brought to the spring because its waters were believed to possess healing virtues. The Priest-King who built the chamber over the spring may not have been aware of the possible virtues of the water, but aware or not, in ordering its construction he had provided not only for the physical but also for the spiritual needs of his guests.

More surprising, perhaps, than the complete drainage systems in the Priest-King's guesthouse and in his residence was the drainage system for the streets of the town, which were equipped with channels on either side. These channels were paved and some of them sunk at least three feet in the ground. One small drain was set in a bed of clay. Drains have been found along the roads that traversed the island. Minoan engineers seem to have been highly skilled in hydraulic science.

If the interpretation of a fragment of painted pottery is correct these engineers also knew how to build fountains. On this fragment what seems to be a jet of water spouts high into the air. Since no one has yet discovered in the island any evidence of a geyser or other natural fountain which the artist might have used as a model one is at liberty to conclude that the design on the fragment of pottery must have been drawn from observation of an artificial one. And artificial fountains were unknown to Egypt or to Greece, at least down to Hellenistic days.

Knossos was not, it is true, the only place in the ancient world where drainage systems had been built. For example, the palace at Tiryns had a bathroom with an escape vent at one end; the island of Melos had a system of conduits, well roofed and paved; and excavations in Palestine have shown that the town of Gezer had a primitive drainage system.

Attempts at sanitation should not surprise anyone who has lived in a warm climate, where people are obliged to learn simple rules of health if they are to survive. The remarkable thing is that in hydraulics the Minoan engineers were so far in advance of the rest of the Mediterranean world.

CHAPTER EIGHT

THE QUEEN'S SUITE

It would be interesting if somewhere on another planet the Queen of France, Marie Antoinette, and her royal cousin, the Queen of Knossos, could meet and compare their recollections of the private suites they lived in while on earth. Marie Antoinette would discover that in one respect her comfort had not been well provided for. She had no bathroom, and the Queen of Knossos had. The Queen of Knossos had other comforts, too. She had a private latrine, fully equipped with seat and flushing facilities.

The Queen's Suite was situated in the magnificent east wing of the Third Palace. It consisted of two apartments: one on the ground floor and one on the floor above, connected with each other by a private staircase. Remnants of this staircase have been found. Of the apartment on the upper floor nothing remains except traces of two latrines and possibly a third.

The apartment on the ground floor comprised a large room, probably the Queen's salon; a small adjoining room about nine feet square, now thought to have been a bathroom; a small latrine equipped with a seat; and another small, windowless room with a raised plaster dais, which may have served as a winter bedroom. The apartment was connected with the service quarter of the palace by a narrow corridor and with the official or royal quarters of the Priest-King by a dark passageway, turning at an angle that has given it the name of the Dog's Leg Corridor.

The large room, or salon, had no windows, but it was sufficiently lighted by two little courts, one to the east, the other to the west. Similar courts were found throughout the palace, some of them large enough to be used as extra rooms. Such courts, usually called light-wells, are characteristic of Minoan architecture. They not only brought light and air into windowless rooms, but they afforded protection against the strong winds which frequently bring heat and dust up from the Sahara Desert. They must also have helped to make life pleasant when chill winter winds blew down from the northwest upon Knossos. Their floors were often paved, their walls brightly colored or adorned with painted reliefs.

The salon itself, thus lighted by its two small courts, was elaborately decorated. Today, except for two modern reproductions of frescoes—the originals are in the Candia Museum— the walls are bare. The Dolphin Fresco, originally painted on the outer wall of the eastern light-well, shows, swimming among other fishes and sea urchins, dolphins with blue backs, pale blue bellies, and orange stripes along their sides. The other fresco, the Dancing Lady, was part of an extensive frieze of dancers which ran around all four walls. The ceiling of the salon was also decorated but with a lotus and papyrus pattern.

Along the walls of the salon stone benches, low enough for short women or for children, were built. In his sketch of the room, as he imagines it may have looked, Monsieur Gilliéron has included a folding stool on which a lady is comfortably seated watching her servant tend a brazier. Gay cushions on the benches, bright frescoes on the walls, and occasional pots of flowers, would have kept the rooms from seeming bare. So many flowerpots were found during the excavations that it seems safe to assume flowers were as popular in Minoan times as they are in modern Crete, where even the humblest home has at least one pot.

The small room adjoining the salon and separated from it by a balustrade was decorated with a frieze, an abstract pattern of running spirals and rosettes, set about halfway up the wall. The spirals were outlined in red against a gray background. Above the spirals fish were painted. Near the entrance to the room remains of a painted terra-cotta tub were lying. When pieced together it was found to be profusely decorated both inside and outside. The interior was painted with tufts of reeds, apparently a set tradition at the time. The exterior was far more elaborate. Above and below a wide central band of conventionalized papyrus pattern a number of wavy lines represent the veins in stonework. Wavy lines were also painted on the rim of the tub.

The proportions of the tub show that it was a hip bath, although grooves for a crossbar, found in similar tubs of an earlier period, are missing here. Many more such hip baths were found in the palace. And they now form one of the most popular exhibits in the Candia Museum. The designs which decorate them are usually tufts of reeds or papyrus, often with waterfowl or fishes swimming among them. Possibly the Egyptian convention of employing designs to indicate the use of the objects decorated influenced the Minoan artist in his choice of patterns.

The bathroom itself had no waste duct as in the well-known bath at Mycenae, where Agamemnon is supposed to have met death at the hands of his queen, Clytemnestra. Nor was there a waste duct in the lavishly decorated hip bath found nearby which is commonly thought of as the royal tub. These tubs must have had to be filled and emptied by hand.

The latrine in the queen's suite is reached by a short corridor connecting the salon with a small light-well known as the Court of the Distaffs because of the distaffs painted on its walls. Light entered the latrine from this court. A groove in one wall shows where the wooden seat could have been fitted in. The underground drains found just below would have insured flushing and ventilation. Evans assigns the latrine and the bathroom to the second half of the Middle Minoan Age of palace construction, perhaps toward the end.

The small light-well, or Court of the Distaffs, is thought to have served as a workroom for the Queen and her ladies. The charming picture in the *Odyssey* of the Phaeacian queen, seated in the hall near the fire, with its light playing over her face while she and her ladies twirl their distaffs of purple wool, may be a reminiscence of Minoan life. The House of the Double Axe had no fireplaces, however; it was heated with braziers that could be carried from room to room. The court of the distaffs was no doubt heated in this way.

The corridor connecting the court with the salon led to the small room Evans calls the Queen's bedroom. The raised dais, oblong in shape, occupies almost the whole of one corner. Covered with soft fleeces, as beds were in Homeric days, the dais would have done well enough for a sleeping place. If the Queen slept here during the winter, in summer she probably retired to the floor above. No other rooms that could have served as sleeping places were found on the ground floor.

Although the suite was separated only by a corridor or so from the central court, the Queen seems to have had no direct access to it. Whether she or her ladies could look down upon the court from their upper rooms is an unanswerable question. If not, then they must have been deprived of much of the life of the palace.

It would be interesting to know whether the Queen, who could have gone through the connecting corridor to the serv-

ice quarter in the rear, was in the habit of using it to inspect
the varied work which was carried on there. Perhaps with her
ladies she sometimes wandered through the closely packed
rooms, seeing long lines of slaves bringing in from the west
wing a steady stream of island products: meats, vegetables,
fruits, and other foods for the household and its many retainers.

The excavations have shown that the service quarter was
very extensive. It housed not only the workers with food sup-
plies but also the potters, goldsmiths, scribes, and other
craftsmen who catered to the needs of the Priest-King's large
establishment. And in addition, it appears to have produced
goods in excess of the Priest-King's needs for export to distant
parts of the Mediterranean world: delicate and gay Minoan
pottery, ivory figurines, necklaces, bracelets, and other luxu-
ries. So many such articles of Minoan craftsmanship have
been found during the excavation of other Mediterranean
sites that Knossos is thought to have carried on a flourishing
export trade emanating from this service wing.

But though the Queen may have felt privileged to enter
the service wing whenever she wished, she doubtless did not
use with quite the same freedom the crooked Dog's Leg
Corridor, which connected her suite with the royal Hall of
the Double Axes. If the evidence can be relied upon that a
gallery ran round this spacious hall where beneath an overhead canopy Minos sat on his golden throne and received his
guests, the ladies of the royal household may have been in-
vited there to watch the brilliant and absorbing scene below.

From the gallery the ladies could also have obtained an
excellent view, through the open portico, of the pine-clad
valley watered by the Kairatos River, where upon festal occasions some of them may have gathered to dance. Though
the Queen and her ladies must have spent much of their time
indoors, out of doors they had plenty to amuse them. They
attended the bull-grappling contests, exciting and awe-in-

spiring; they were not excluded from the theater as Athenian ladies were; and some of them shared the hunting expeditions of their men. They enjoyed themselves, these gay ladies of bygone days in Minoan Crete.

It is a pity that the name of Pasiphaë, mother of Ariadne and of the Bull-man, has alone survived the destruction of the ages. For it would be good to know of the other queens, more worthy, who lived out their lives in the luxury of the suite in the east wing.

CHAPTER NINE

THE PRIEST-KING'S PEOPLE

Some think that the prehistoric inhabitants of Crete were an indigenous people; others that they came from Cilicia. Those who believe in their Cilician origin base their argument partly upon the Anatolian character of the names Talos, Minos, and Knossos, partly upon the similarity in Crete and in Cilicia between certain religious practices, especially their reverence for the double axe as a sacred emblem. Although their earliest cultural ties may have been with the eastern coast of the Mediterranean—Zeus went there to find a wife—the people still owed much of their development to their increasing contact with the Nile Valley.

To discover the physical characteristics of bygone races anthropologists turn to skeletons. They can call upon architecture, sculpture, pottery, and the minor arts to support some of their conclusions, but it is upon bony structure they rely. It must have been rather frustrating to Evans, then, that he was unable to find in any of the Minoan tombs, coffins, or burial jars a complete adult skeleton. Bones were everywhere, in charnel houses, in caves, under the floors of dwelling houses, but nowhere an adult skeleton with all its parts intact. Evans and his anthropologist friends had to be content with separate bones and with skulls.

They examined the long bones of the skeletons first. After careful measurements and comparisons they concluded that the average height of the prehistoric inhabitants of the island was some two inches shorter than that of the present inhabitants. This would make them about five feet and four inches tall. They were also a small-boned race. From this the anthropologists drew the conclusion that the Minoans must have depended on brain and agility of limb rather than on weight or size of body.

Skull measurement also entered into the picture, for the shape of a man's skull, and particularly the cephalic index, or the relation between its breadth and its length, have much to tell of his origins. The evidence showed that the Minoans could not have remained an isolated people. Others must have found the island a pleasant and profitable place to live in, whether they came as hostile invaders or as immigrants. The gradual influx that occurred over the centuries caused a visible modification of the early longheaded, or dolichocephalic type, as the measurements of the skulls showed. The Cretans of today are, for the most part, mesocephalic; that is, they have achieved a nice balance between the early longheads and the broadheads, or brachycephalic type, that appeared later on the island.

Various theories have been offered to account for this modification of the physical type, which seems to have taken place during the Late Minoan Age. Scholars know that the Mediterranean type, to which the Libyans and the Egyptians belonged, was originally longheaded and that the bulk of the Cretans belonged to this stock, but they do not know whether the marked change that occurred in the later population was the result of mixed marriages or whether the new conditions of life were sufficient to cause a change. Some think the tremendous falling off of the longheads was caused by hostile invaders, possibly from the north. Others attribute this ousting of the longheads to the driving back of the old Mediterranean stock by the Indo-Europeans. Another theory attributes the change to the early intrusion of the Alpine Man from the north.

Measurement of bones, however suggestive, does not tell the whole story. The painted likenesses of Minoan men and women still live in the frescoes. Fragments though they are, they can tell more about themselves than most people can learn from the dry bones so carefully studied by the anthropologists.

The Cup-bearer is considered a typical example of the mingling of longheads with broadheads. In other words, he is a modern young Cretan, and his like may be seen everywhere on the island. Armenoid in type, he resembles the two portrait heads that may represent an ancient Priest-King and his young son. If at one time the dominant ethnic element on the island was Armenoid, skulls like the Cup-bearer's may have come from a mixture of the early Mediterranean longheads with the Armenoid type of southwest Anatolia and Syria.

The Cup-bearer has an unusually slender waist. As the excavations progressed trim waists were found to be characteristic of the Minoans. Whether they were naturally a slender-waisted folk, and the artist has accentuated this feature, or whether the waist was artificially contracted, as the feet of a wellborn Chinese girl once were, was at first the subject of much argument. Evans has suggested that the small waist of the Minoans was an actual physical characteristic and not a matter of artistic convention, but that it had been produced by mechanical devices. At some stage in the child's growth, he believes, perhaps between the ages of six and ten, a tight padded belt, plated with metal, was put around his waist, to remain there throughout his life. If this is true it is true only for boys in early Cretan custom. The figurines of Neolithic women show no constriction of the waist; rather, the opposite. And one early figurine shows a woman potter with a natural waist. An ivory half-cylinder of later date portrays a man and a woman who stand facing each other. The man's waist is extraordinarily narrow; the woman has no waist at all. It seems reasonable to suggest, then, that men wore tight belts before women began to imitate them, a young boy being put into a belt when he became old enough for a loincloth. This suggestion is strengthened by evidence that narrow waists did not become a feminine fashion until the seventeenth century B.C. Perhaps at this period young girls adopted the tight belt.

The first thought that occurs to one today is whether this interference with the course of nature tended to produce ill effects, especially in women. But the medical authorities who were consulted by Evans seem to have felt that such artificial constriction need not necessarily have been harmful to physical health.

Elderly men may have discarded the metal belt in favor of one made of leather and of more ample proportions. The evidence for this supposition depends chiefly upon the interpretation of a figure on a vase from Hagia Triada. Here an old man leads a group of reapers or, as some think, a procession of dancers. His loose belt of leather and his ecstatic face create the impression that he has never been so comfortable in all his life. The facial expressions of two bronze figurines, representing Minoan men of heavy build, are not as easily interpreted, but their loose belts are clearly visible.

Minoan men were not only trim of figure; they were usually clean-shaven, and until about the sixteenth century they wore their dark hair short. When beards are portrayed in Minoan art the individuals represented are either foreigners or persons influenced by Libyan fashion. For Libyan men, it appears, wore a sort of goatee. To achieve a clean-shaven effect something more than the blunt edge of a primitive bronze razor must surely have been needed, and this need may have been met by using a tweezer similar to one found in a grave on the island of Mochlos. Tweezers may, of course, have been used by Minoan women, if not to pluck their eyebrows, then in other ways in order to beautify their persons.

The physical appearance of the women, like that of the men, is surprisingly unlike that of the ancient Greeks. The Greek profile, in which the nose is a prolongation of the forehead, never appears in Minoan art. The Minoan forehead is straight. From it the nose springs abruptly. Its tip, especially when a woman is being portrayed, is often slightly retroussé, giving to its owner a somewhat impudent air.

If the Cup-bearer is a member of the Minoan aristocracy *La Parisienne* can claim the same distinction. Her curls are arranged, rather artificially for the modern taste, in a row across her straight forehead; other curls partially conceal her small well-set ears, and the rest of her hair is held in place by a ribbon. The wide-open eyes, well-shaped mouth with its full, red lips, the body with its slender waist and curving hips all create the impression of an individual who is the finished product of past generations. With her friends she strolls on the terrace of her southern home, plucking a flower for her hair; on festival days she is seated with her mother in the front row of the spectators who have gathered in the arena to watch the game, poised and confident, even though she is in the presence of men.

That Minoan civilization, even at its height, was capable of producing so exquisite a type of womanhood as *La Parisienne* is as startling to museum-goers as it was to the excavators when they first unearthed her painted image from centuries of accumulated debris. Unlike her later Greek sister of the mainland, she appears to be a person accustomed not only to a life of greater freedom but to one of greater luxury as well, the kind of life the world would not see again for many a century to come.

In stature Minoan women, like the men, were inclined to be short rather than tall, slender of build, and apparently fair in complexion. Their heads were long compared with their breadth, their features well-shaped, and their chins good. Their hair and eyes were as brilliantly dark as those of a Neapolitan or Sicilian of today.

Among the rather delicately built Minoan figures in the frescoes a small number appear which suggest the presence of a very alien group on the island. This group may be represented, it has been suggested, by the Negroid figures on the Town-mosaic. These figures exist only in fragments, but the swarthy color of the skin and the prominence of the lower jaw render this suggestion a likely one. Negroid figures also appear on a pendant for a gold necklace. And in a fresco known as the Captain of the Blacks a spirited youth is followed closely by negro troops. The youth is garbed in much the same fashion as the Cup-bearer and other processional figures. Immediately behind him a black follows, dressed in a similar uniform, his lieutenant, perhaps, or officer in charge of the troops who follow at a smart trot. The fresco is thought to represent a squad of black mercenaries who acted as palace guards, in imitation of the Egyptian practice of using Libyans in a like capacity. If the interpretation of these Negroid figures is correct an African strain may have been introduced at an early period into the Minoan population of Crete, though there is no evidence in the representations surviving.

Minoan art has portrayed for the modern world a people whose physical appearance is now as well known to museum-goers as that of the ancient Egyptians. Perhaps Minoan art has something to say also about the mental and emotional characteristics of the Priest-King's people.

In the first place, the Minoans do not seem to have been a

war-loving people. Numbers of swords, short daggers, arrow-heads, and other weapons have been found, but this need not mean that the islanders were themselves warlike. The young man on the ivory half-cylinder who may be celebrating his marriage wears a dagger thrust into his belt to defend himself in time of war, a custom familiar to all from the old Scottish habit of carrying a dagger or a knife thrust into the top of a stocking. In the frescoes and vase paintings scenes of a peaceful nature predominate; only in the later period of deterioration do a few warlike scenes occur. The shape and size of the great shields in these scenes may indicate that they were constructed for defense rather than offense. None of this, naturally, can be regarded as conclusive proof, but judging from what has survived, the glorification of war could not have been a theme for artistic expression.

The Minoans do seem, on the other hand, to have been a daring and vigorous people, independent, individualistic, and yet gregarious. The favorite sport of both sexes was bull-grappling and a close second stalking wild bulls. In the frescoes and on seals we see both men and women portrayed, standing erect in their chariots, presumably to hunt wild animals. At the public spectacles women occupy the front seats, with the men standing behind them.

They show their individualism in various ways. In their art they are never mere slavish imitators; like the later Greeks, when they take what others have to offer they imbue it with life, with grace, and with beauty. They plan their towns along definite lines, but they build their houses as they choose, apparently without regard to symmetry, holding convenience of greater importance. All these things can be safely inferred from the handiwork they have left behind them, even though no literature exists to support the inference.

They were fond of bright colors. Even in early days they covered the inside walls of their houses with painted plaster, doubtless utilitarian in origin but affording satisfaction to the eye. They must have loved flowers, for flowers appear every-where, painted on delicate vases, on alabaster cups, even on bathtubs, although here aquatic plants are more apt to be found. The lily, the iris, and the crocus recur again and again, the lily especially, in exquisite sprays painted with fidelity to nature, with restraint, and with appreciation.

They had a sense of humor. On a Middle Minoan signet a puckish-looking imp with grinning mouth and curved horns raises his hands in surprise. On a sealing a flat-headed Mino-taur seems to be eating his own hand. And on another sealing a winged cherub is shown with lion's feet. Hogarth has sug-gested a reason for this display of wry humor; the need to baffle forgers of seals by constantly ringing the changes on a limited number of seal-types. Of particular interest is a round-faced goblin, with flaring ears modeled on the flanges of a double axe.

Imagination, originality, inventiveness are other character-istics that can be ascribed to the prehistoric inhabitants of the island. These characteristics appear in the fantastic shapes of their pottery, in their engraved seal-stones, in their beautiful jewelry, and in the delicacy of their carved ivory, many ex-amples of which are to be seen in museums. The same charac-teristics also appear in full measure in the frescoes and in the ornamental friezes that served as architectual adornment. Whether the artist is portraying the human figure, as in the ivory Bull-leaper, or an animal, as in the remarkable fresco in which a cat is stalking a pheasant, he works with a freedom and a grace unexcelled until a far later day.

That the Priest-King's people were religious is evident from the frequent representations of religious practices in their art. Expressed in symbols of an often crude anthropomorphic and prehistoric realism, motivated by fear and terror and the need to placate the unknown, but also stirred by a sense of awe and even ecstatic adoration before the Mother Goddess, their religion exerted a strong influence upon the religious thought and practices of Greece.

Whatever the origin of the Priest-King's people, whether they were indigenous or an Anatolian people who brought with them from Cilicia the worship of a mother goddess, the island of Crete early became the melting pot of the Mediterranean. So mixed, they came to be gifted and versatile people, original and independent, and quickly made their island the seat of a unique civilization.

CHAPTER TEN

KNOSSOS, MISTRESS OF THE SEA

The great city crowned by its Priest-King's palace, which the archaeologists have found and peopled for the world, had become in its Golden Age the heart of a maritime empire. Gradually the rulers of Knossos had succeeded in establishing in the Mediterranean world the peace which is always a vital necessity to an empire built on trade. Minoan fleets had swept the sea so free of pirates that traders could move safely from port to port, not only to exchange wares with other peoples, but to learn new ways of life. Attracted by what Crete had to offer, foreign traders put in at her ports. Egypt had made her acquaintance as early as the Neolithic age. Professor Caskey, the Director of the American School of Classical Studies at Athens, during his excavation of Lerna on the Greek mainland, uncovered evidence that in the Middle Bronze Age (roughly the Second Millennium) Crete and Lerna had enjoyed considerable contact with each other.

Relations with Cyprus were both happy and profitable. Minoan ships visited the settlements along the coast of Asia

Minor and exchanged wares with the inhabitants. To Pylos in southern Greece, where King Nestor of Homeric fame once lived, these prehistoric Cretans journeyed in their primitive boats, and there or at Mycenae they may have seen the amber that came from the faraway north. Crete has never produced either tin or silver, and until she learned to manufacture bronze what little she had was imported and therefore costly. For its manufacture she had to import tin, perhaps from Cornwall. She mixed her tin with copper from Cyprus, smelted the two ores together, and produced enough bronze for her needs. From then on she made rapid progress.

Contact between Crete and Egypt was especially fruitful during Crete's Middle Minoan Age. This period corresponds, roughly, to Egypt's Middle Kingdom, from about 2100 to about 1700 B.C. During this time Egypt expanded both to the north and to the south. Commerce between the two countries increased steadily and with benefit to both. The seated statue of an Egyptian was found in Crete, and in the service of the Pharaohs, Minoan architects and engineers went to Egypt.

The material prosperity of Knossos during the Golden Age, which is reflected in all branches of art, seems to have been spurred on by the severe earthquake of 1700. For Knossos could not be deterred by earthquakes, whether or not she believed, with other early cultures, that they were caused by a mighty beast, bellowing beneath the earth. Though in the course of the excavations only two major earthquakes were surely found to have made their utterly disastrous marks, there must have been many more if the number which have occurred on the island in recent centuries—thirty from the thirteenth through the nineteenth centuries A.D.—can be considered as a sign. The region round Knossos has always been particularly hurt by them, for the eastern part of the island, where Knossos lies, is by its geological structure especially subject to them. Certainly Knossos had coped with earthquakes before. And after that which late in the Middle

Minoan Age leveled her magnificence she again plucked up her courage to rebuild, and to rebuild more strongly. Settlements increased and road communications improved. Tombs for the dead were no longer merely cut from the soft rock that could so easily collapse; many were built of stone blocks that must have seemed at the time sufficiently durable to withstand the fury of nature.

As the city of Knossos grew in extent and in population she began to reach out for larger and larger markets. It sounds almost too modern to attribute the expansion of a prehistoric city to industrial revolution, and yet the industrial revolution that spread from Knossos over the island as the manufacture of bronze grew in importance was probably the largest factor in the city's remarkable growth. Caravans coming from the north or the east, along the ancient amber route from Britain to the east, soon found in Crete not only a good market in which to dispose of their wares, but an excellent center from which the new alloy could be distributed to other markets in the Mediterranean. With a shrewd eye to the future the Priest-Kings of Knossos had early set themselves to the task of equipping and maintaining a fleet of ships in which to import what they needed in the way of raw materials and to export their own finished products to other lands.

Knossos was not without rivals both at home and abroad. Nor was Knossos the only large city on the island. Mallia to the east, Phaestus and Hagia Triada to the southwest had all come to be important centers of Minoan culture and art. Early in the Middle Minoan Age, roughly about 2000 B.C., Knossos, Mallia, and Phaestus were rich and powerful enough for their rulers to erect great palaces in which to gather together their families, their retainers, and the petty officials who helped to administer the royal properties. Wealthy citizens built houses of several stories, with oil presses and storage chambers on the ground floors. Paved streets, running water, and other amenities of civilized life that are taken for granted today existed in all these cities.

Phaestus, in particular, which was situated in a dominating position with easy access to the Libyan Sea, soon began to rival Knossos in power and wealth. Unlike Knossos, which is located in a narrow valley, Phaestus rises about three hundred feet above a wide plain. And Phaestus, like Knossos, had no circuit walls but depended on the massive walls of its palace. Rivalry between the two cities increased steadily, and for a time control of the island shifted back and forth from one to the other.

In Phaestus, which was excavated in the nineteenth century by the French, a discovery of unusual importance was made: the celebrated Phaestus Disk, now carefully preserved in the Candia Museum. The disk can be best described as a round, flat clay tablet somewhat larger than a dinner plate. Its chief significance lies in its being the earliest inscribed document found in Crete. Although the experts agreed that the strange signs, shaped differently from those at Knossos and arranged in spirals round the center, had been impressed by means of stamps or dies between the eighteenth and seventeenth centuries, they could not agree upon the meaning of the signs. Some think they refer to a sea raid or possibly a treaty; one scholar, that they form a music score. It would be interesting indeed if at some future date scholars were to discover that the disk contained a treaty made between Phaestus and Knossos referring to a common use of ports.

Between Knossos and Mallia on the site of the harbor town of Nirou Khani, Evans and Xanthudides excavated in 1919 a large stone building which proved to be an almost equally remarkable find. For on its walls they saw painted religious emblems, double axes, and bull's horns, and in the building itself—it consisted of some forty rooms—they found between forty and fifty tripod altars. As they progressed with their task they came upon other ritual objects, among them a cylinder showing a ship under full sail. And when they found that the town had been a flourishing manufacturing and artistic center as well as a port they concluded that this unusually large building had been designed for the production and shipping overseas of ritual vessels, either to keep religious beliefs alive in the hearts of Minoan colonists or to propagate the faith.

Mallia was itself an important port, and because of its excellent location at the terminus of a road from eastern Crete it must have handled a great deal of trade. A steady growth of overseas as well as domestic trade brought such prosperity to Mallia that by the Middle Minoan Age the Priest-King's palace bade fair to equal that of Knossos itself. To Mallia's ruler may have belonged a ceremonial axe, its butt carved to resemble a leopard, and a magnificient sword, both found among the ruins. The sword, obviously a sword of state, is almost a meter in length, longer than any other sword of the period. Its hilt is of ivory plated with gold and its knob rock crystal set with amethyst. And to Mallia's queen may have belonged an exquisite piece of jewelry: a gold pendant formed by a single cluster of what appear to be bees.

Knossos, although without a port exclusively her own and beset by rivals, in the end gained complete control of the island. By means of a network of roads radiating out from the city her priest-kings could go easily and quickly from one part of the island to the other. What is thought to be the oldest road in Europe forms a part of this intricate road system of ancient Crete. Paved along its entire length and flanked on both sides by well-constructed drains, it formed the state approach to the House of the Double Axe. As yet, no marks of wheel traffic have been found on this Royal Road, and the lack of wheel marks has led to the assumption that it was intended for the litters in which the palace officials traveled.

In addition to the royal road, other roads were set apart

for official use. For the common public and for the ordinary traffic of the island a separate road system was built and maintained, fully protected at strategic points by defensive works. One of these roads, raised above the ground to a height of some thirty feet, led across a viaduct. Its massive piers, now unearthed, are a tribute to Minoan engineering skill. These well-constructed roads, increasing in extent and in number over the years, helped greatly to strengthen the Priest-King's power in the island.

After the earthquake of the Middle Minoan Age the House of the Double Axe was restored; its workshops again hummed with activity, and trade again flourished. Egypt, however, had fallen into political difficulties, and her markets were for a time closed to Minoan merchants. But the East remained open; and in that direction Minoan ships built up their trade, bringing back to the island, among other importations, a strange new animal, the horse. From the East came the chariot, too. Probably the Minoan people soon became accustomed to the sight of their betters riding along the paved roads in chariots drawn by animals rather than in litters carried by men. That chariots and horses did come to be numerous in the island is proved by the royal inventories. In Greek art horses have long, flowing manes, but this was not the fashion in Minoan Crete. The manes of Minoan horses were carefully divided into three tufts and each one knotted.

Thriving traffic with the East caused traders to establish themselves along the coast of the Mediterranean and on the adjacent islands. Under Minoan influence a school of art sprang up on the island of Cyprus, and its artistic products soon came to rival those of Knossos itself. The silver Crete had always lacked now began to flow in from the Cilician mainland, and the art of the silversmith grew in importance. Minoan ships also brought in the saffron crocus. The cultivation of this plant became a source of wealth to the priest-kings of Knossos. Almost overnight Minoan taste in colors

99

changed. Saffron became the fashionable color, one might almost say the royal color, so constantly did it appear in court circles. When Crete came under Venetian control in 1204 A.D. the cultivation of saffron was revived; and today saffron gardens still flourish in the island.

With the growth of industry at home and the expansion of trade overseas it was inevitable that wealth and power should center more and more in the hands of a minority. But in Knossos the people also prospered; for the rise in prosperity affected the whole city. Society was slowly transformed. Urban life superseded the old ways under the impact of the larger Mediterranean world, especially Egypt and Libya. This is shown in a variety of ways. For example, the Libyan fashion of wearing the hair in long side-locks seems to have appealed to Minoan men; so they began to let their hair grow. Fashions in dress, particularly for women, became more sophisticated. The single garment of the past gradually evolved into a jacket and skirt, surprisingly modern in appearance, which remained until the end the distinctive dress of a Minoan woman.

Burial customs also changed. Hitherto whole families had been put to rest in a common charnel house, doubtless that the members of a family might remain together and meet again in the life beyond. Although families continued to bury infants and very young children in jars beneath the floors of their houses, adults were now carried outside the city, where rock-cut tombs awaited the painted coffins in which the dead had been sealed. Many of these tombs, when opened, proved to have been rifled long ago of the gifts that once must have been brought there to comfort and sustain the soul on its journey to the After World. Enough remained in some of them to indicate the growing prosperity of the island and the changes that were taking place in the social fabric of Minoan Crete.

The Priest-King of Knossos now lived on a magnificent

scale. The new prosperity made itself felt in the palace area to a far greater extent than ever before. In the great courts of the House of the Double Axe stone theaters with tiers of seats for the spectators were erected. Here many public spectacles took place. Although the Little Palace was built presumably to placate the underworld powers it may also have served as a prehistoric Petit Trianon, to pleasure the Priest-King in his leisure hours.

A Royal Villa, too, was erected, with several stairways leading to an upper story from which the Priest-King could enjoy an excellent view of the Kairatos River. The situation of this villa must have been delightful. With its wide terraces, its many windows, and its balustraded balconies, where the women of the household could gather for conversation, the royal villa fully deserved its name.

In the past Crete had always been more open to southern than to northern influence. Not until the Golden Age did Knossos begin to cast covetous eyes upon the mainland of Greece that stretched invitingly down from the north. Soon Minoan ships, laden with exports, began to sail to the smaller islands that lay just beyond Crete. Settlers followed, at first in small numbers, then, growing bolder, in larger and larger groups. This movement toward the north is associated in the minds of some scholars with the rapid rise to power in Knossos of that semi-mythical king, Minos. Whether he is to be known by this name or by some other, it is clear that by this time the ruling Priest-King had gained complete control of the Mediterranean and was now able to move in whatever direction he wished.

When Knossos became the seat of a strong sea empire the House of the Double Axe became the true center of the island's administration. No longer did the Priest-King need even a mechanical man to patrol his coast. Riding in his sedan chair (there is a miniature model of one in the Candia Museum) over the excellent road system he had built, he could go easily and comfortably to any point on the island. These roads, reaching their climax in the Golden Age, are thought by many scholars to be important clues to the surprising uniformity of culture that the excavations have shown existed throughout the whole of Crete.

What Crete had learned from Egypt and her other neighbors she had by this time absorbed and made her own, so quickly outstripping her teachers that the pupils must be credited with an unusually large share both of natural endowment and of spiritual energy. These gifts Crete has never lost.

The discovery of Knossos has meant much to the world of scholarship; it has also meant much to artists and to craftsmen; but it has meant even more to those who live on the island, for now they can—and do—look back with pride to the established fact that they also have made their contribution to the culture of the world.

PART TWO

MINOAN LIFE
AND CUSTOMS

CHAPTER ONE

THE MINOAN FAMILY

The Minoan family was, at first, not a family at all; it was a clan group housed under one roof. The discovery of the foundations of several large houses in Knossos, to which additions on the ground floor of small, cell-like rooms had obviously been made, points to the housing either of exceptionally big families or of clan groups. The adding of small rooms is regarded as evidence that these houses were intended for such groups and not for individual families, and that when a member of the group married he brought his bride home to live with him in one of the cell-like rooms built especially for him. The tall houses of several stories whose fronts appear in miniature on the Town-mosaic may have served the same purpose, although for this supposition there is no evidence. The historians say that about the sixteenth century B.C. the clans were breaking up in the Aegean world and that individual households were becoming the rule rather than the exception. This agrees with the finds of the archaeologists in Knossos.

To inquire into the nature of an individual Minoan household or family and to discover how it was equipped for daily life is a fascinating study.

The most important event in the common life of a new household is the arrival of its first child. To the primitive mind birth is a mystery. Nor has the sexual act, to the primitive mind, any connection with birth. Mark Twain has pictured the amazement of Adam when he returned one day to his cave and found there beside Eve a strange creature he had never seen before. Eve said it was hers, and with that Adam had to be content. A Minoan mother may have given the same answer, until the facts of paternity were known. After the facts of paternity were understood some scholars think that female superiority came to an end. However that may be, the arrival of a child, particularly if it happened to be a boy, in any early household would be an important event, since he would soon become a valuable economic asset. And in a community where a bride brings a fair price a girl, too, would be an asset.

If an expectant mother needed assistance in giving birth to her child she may have turned to dittany, a plant native to Crete and believed by the historic Greeks to be highly efficacious in childbirth. Some scholars think that the large number of Greek birth-goddesses whose origins have been traced to Crete points to difficulties at childbirth which women may sometimes have felt as a result of mixed marriages. Others hold that the belief may have sprung from the custom of calling in a midwife.

The practice of midwifery was so widespread in the ancient world that though history is silent on Cretan midwives it seems safe to assume their existence. Folk tales indicate their activity. They knew many devices, usually magical, to hasten or retard delivery; to hasten delivery, they said, all knots must be untied; to retard it, all knots must be carefully tied. One story of the birth of Heracles reveals another method of retarding delivery. Eileithyia, in origin a Cretan birth-goddess,

sat for seven days and seven nights, so the tale runs, outside
Alcmene's door. During all this time she kept her hands
tightly clasped about her knees. Only when a waiting woman
tricked the goddess into springing up from her crouched position was Alcmene safely delivered of her son.

Children born into a Minoan household were doubtless
treated just as they were elsewhere in the Mediterranean
world. Legend relates that the newly born Zeus was bathed
in a river and then swaddled. The late author, Apollodorus,
adds that the child was guarded by the mythical Kouretes,
who clashed their shields together to prevent his cries from
being overheard. Aristotle approved wholeheartedly of bath-
ing newborn infants in cold water, preferably river water.
Spartan mothers bathed their infants in wine, to test their
constitutions. The weak were thrown into convulsions; the
strong survived. Spartan mothers did not follow the almost
universal custom which Aristotle also approved of; he thought
that swaddling kept a baby's soft limbs from becoming
twisted. Perhaps a Spartan mother thought that if a child's
limbs were so weak that they needed to be bound in swaddling clothes, he had better not be reared at all.

Since in the lower cultures loud noises are supposed to
drive away any demons who may be hovering about, the
clashing noises made by the Kouretes may reflect an actual
custom on the part of human parents anxious to protect their
babies from attack by the forces of evil. That young children
were thought to need special protection against evil was probably true among the Minoans as among other early peoples.
Indeed this belief has not yet died out in certain parts of
the world. Even today in both Greece and Turkey blue beads
are often tied into a child's hair, the color blue being regarded
as a powerful prophylactic. Shells, as symbols of life, are
also good magic. Although shell amulets have not been
found in the excavations at Knossos or anywhere else in
Crete a great many made of other material have been un-

earthed. Neolithic strata have yielded amulets made of pebbles. In Minoan days lapis lazuli, rock crystal, magnetite, chalcedony, and gold seem to have been favored for amulets, although others, made of less durable material, may not have survived. Many of these amulets are shaped like parts of the body, generally the leg or the arm. Others are in the shape of fish, lions, ducks, toads, or in one instance, a miniature axe. Some are perforated, doubtless to be worn as pendants. Probably not only Minoan children but their elders as well were protected by the constant wearing of an amulet.

It may, then, be assumed that the new arrival in a Minoan household was bathed, protected against evil by every possible means, and swaddled so tightly that he would be unable to move any part of his body except his head, and that he would remain in this unnatural state until his limbs were strong enough for him to move about freely. At the age of ten, or even younger, his small waist would be encircled by a metal belt. Most of his early infancy he probably spent strapped to his mother's back, or to the back of an older child in the family. This is still the custom in many Oriental countries, where children play about with infants strapped to their backs, apparently unhampered by their burdens.

Tradition says that three of the infant gods, Zeus, Dionysus, and Hermes, were provided with cradles. Zeus's cradle was suspended from the branch of a tree and gently rocked by errant breezes. Dionysus was put into a winnowing fan: a broad basket for separating the grain from the chaff. Hermes had a special kind of portable cradle. And the infant Heracles was cradled in his father's shield, as befitted the son of a warrior. Doubtless young Minoans were also placed in cradles, if only to relieve some tired back.

Nothing is known about the diet of young children. A legend, often discounted, relates that the infant Zeus was fed on milk and honey. The milk came from the goat, Amaltheia, who suckled the newborn child. A variant of the legend says that the milk came from a cow. On late coins both animals are shown giving suck to the infant god, the goat appearing more often than the cow. Older children were, it seems likely, fed as the young Achilles was in the *Iliad,* on tender meat, marrow, relishes, fat, and wine.

Among some ancient peoples an unwanted child was quickly disposed of, especially if he seemed to be a weakling. If he were strong and healthy he would be an asset rather than a liability, even though he would be an extra mouth to feed. The goddess Hera wanted to conceal her child, Hephaestus, when she saw that he had been born lame. To the modern mind infanticide is a horrifying thought; to the ancient mind it was often a bitter economic necessity. The chances are strong that even in relatively prosperous Minoan Crete a deformed infant, or a sickly one, was not reared but was disposed of in some way.

For amusement young children, before they were old enough to work, must have been thrown largely upon themselves. A chamber tomb from one of the cemeteries near Knossos has yielded several small objects that may be children's toys, perhaps to be taken with them to the After World. The infant Zeus, according to legend, had a many-colored ball to play with. And it may be recalled that the young princess, Nausicaä, played ball with her maidens while they waited for the wind and the sun to dry the family laundry they had just washed in a running stream.

Children in historic Greece had various ways of amusing themselves, and since childish games are more or less alike the world over, at least when children are left to themselves, Minoan children must have known what to do with their leisure hours. Perhaps, like little Pheidippides in *The Clouds* of Aristophanes, they carved boats, made chariots out of leather, and frogs out of pomegranate rinds. "Young things," says Aristotle, "can not keep still."

The little that has been learned about Minoan marriage

customs has been gleaned from two scenes. One is engraved on the ivory half-cylinder found near Knossos; the other forms part of a fresco known as the Jewel Fresco. Although both the cylinder and the fresco belong to approximately the same period of Minoan civilization and have been interpreted as possibly referring to betrothal or marriage, the two scenes portray persons who are so unlike each other in every particular that the temptation is strong to regard them as belonging to entirely different walks in life.

The scene on the ivory half-cylinder might be a form of betrothal or marriage ceremony. Facing each other and with right hands clasped, stand a man and a woman. The woman wears an ungirdled dress that falls straight from her shoulders to a point midway between knee and ankle. Her bare feet are placed modestly side by side. The man wears the usual loincloth and a dagger in his belt. He stands with his right foot well advanced. His left arm hangs stiffly at his side, the thumb pointing downward. The artist has not attempted to show the woman's left arm or hand. The right arm of each figure, however, is sharply bent at the elbow so that the forearms almost touch. Neither participant in this ceremony wears trinkets of any kind. The woman's hair hangs well below her shoulders with no fillet or band to hold it in place. No necklaces, bracelets, or even anklets are worn by either the man or the woman. Such simplicity is remarkable in a people who loved to adorn their persons on all occasions.

In the Jewel Fresco a man stands behind a seated woman who is elegantly dressed. He seems to be fastening around her throat a gold necklace to which a piece of blue material is attached. Although only a fragment of this scene remains Evans suggests that it may represent a wedding ceremony. The blue material, he thinks, resembles that of *La Parisienne's* butterfly bow and the other knots associated with Minoan religion.

The two scenes, granted always that they refer to marriage,

may possibly be the artist's portrayal of the various parts of a ceremony. But it seems more likely that he may be portraying on the half-cylinder a simple ceremony between two persons in a lower walk of life, while the fresco represents a more elaborate ceremony in which the piece of blue material, if it means anything, emphasizes the religious side.

Today in Greece the requirement of a dowry is of long standing, and many a young woman remains unmarried because the dowry asked for is beyond her means. This situation could never have risen in the earlier Minoan world, where marriage was an economic necessity.

In pre-Hellenic days a new household was provided with fire from a parental hearth. Burning charcoal was ceremoniously carried from the old establishment to the new one, or a torch was lighted at the old hearth and carried to the new— an important ceremony, for in an era before flint or matches, to let a fire go out would be a serious matter. This custom of carrying the fire may also have existed in prehistoric Crete. A tripod hearth, found tightly sealed in the shrine of a private house in Knossos, contained charcoal ashes. If Carbon 14 had been known when Evans discovered the hearth, he would have been able to date it more accurately. However, using such means as he had at hand and comparing his new find with other tripod hearths previously found on the site, he came to the conclusion that since it did not resemble any of them it might have served to carry burning embers from an old home to a new one. Otherwise, there seemed to be no reason for its having been sealed.

At this point two interesting questions come to mind. If, as in historic Greece, a deceased member of the family was believed to appear on occasion in serpent form, what happened when a new household was set up? Did he desert the old household and attach himself to the new, or did he favor them both with his appearances? These are nice questions but, like other questions related to prehistoric life in Crete, impossible to answer.

The separate house in which a newly married couple lived might be oval in shape, round, or rectangular. It might have a door and a window or only a door. The foundations of an oval house in the town of Chamaesi in eastern Crete contained a number of square rooms built around a small open patio. It seems to have had no entrance on the ground floor but was entered from the top either by a bridge or by a ladder that could be drawn up at night. Somewhat similar houses can still be seen in the Middle East.

The round, or tower, houses in Crete also had to be entered from the top. In spite of these traces of both oval and round houses, it is generally agreed that even in Neolithic days the prevailing type of dwelling was rectangular. The belief that rectangular houses continued to be preferred is based partly upon the shape of Minoan chamber tombs. Entrance to these tombs was through a rectangular room that communicated at the rear with an inner chamber where the dead were placed. And since, as is also generally agreed, the houses of the dead are often modeled upon those of the living it has been suggested that this may have been true in Minoan Crete.

Gournia, southeast of Knossos, is the best surviving example of a small prehistoric Cretan town. Here excavations showed that middle- and upper-class families occupied houses of more than one story with rooms usually grouped around a patio. Houses built on a slope had basement rooms with a back-door entrance. The front entrance was flush with the street. Many of these houses contained from six to twelve rooms, occasionally more. Separate quarters for men and women do not seem to have existed in Gournia.

The houses of less prosperous people seem to have been one-storied with only two or three small rooms set around a small court. Probably the entire family slept on the bare earthen floor or at best upon the skins of goats or the fleeces of sheep. Although in Knossos the better houses had bathtubs, in the houses of the poor such refinements of living were as unknown as they are today in Crete.

The heating of houses in a southern climate never presents as much of a problem as it does in a northern climate. The discovery of fixed hearths in some of the earlier houses and of movable clay fireboxes in later ones, including one in the Hall of the Double Axes, indicates that the fixed hearth was gradually given up in favor of the clay firebox, since the latter could be moved about from room to room. During the summer the family, like most southern peoples today, perhaps remained indoors to escape the noonday sun or slept in the shade of a tree until the dangerous rays of the sun had weakened. During the short winter or when cold winds blew from the north the house could be heated, or at least the chill removed, by means of this ancient prototype of the Oriental brazier. Since there is no evidence of chimneys in Minoan houses, the smoke would have had to escape through a door or through the open light-well.

These braziers may sometimes have been used for cooking. In Chile if an *inquilina* housewife is prevented by rain from doing her cooking outside, she lights a small fire on the earthen floor of her house, sets her pot over it, and proceeds with her work, undisturbed by the smoke that escapes as best it can through an open door or window. Sometimes a Minoan housewife may also have had to cook indoors. It is, of course, possible that a well-to-do family set aside a separate room for cooking. Evans suggests that a small room in the east wing of the Third Palace may have been used as a kitchen. A stone shelf covered with fine white plaster runs along an inner wall of the room, and in the center of the shelf a depression large enough for a charcoal fire has been hollowed out. Below the shelf are two steps. A person standing on the upper step could easily prepare a meal over the fire. A separate room for cooking would, however, be un-known in the average Minoan household.

The interior of a Minoan house might have seemed bare to western, but not to eastern, eyes. The West crowds its rooms with furniture; the Orient is content with a greater simplicity. We know a good deal about early Egyptian household furniture, because Egypt has been relatively untroubled by earthquakes and because Egyptian air is dry. But unfortu-nately the air of Crete is not dry, and Crete has not been untroubled by earthquakes. What the earthquakes in Crete spared, the moist air gradually destroyed. Nevertheless, scholars have amassed a respectable amount of knowledge about Minoan furniture and other articles of household use.

Stone benches that served as seats and stone platforms that may have served as sleeping places can still be seen in the Third Palace. Remains of the wooden chest in the sides of which were set the panels of fine-glazed clay representing Minoan house-fronts, show the good craftsmanship that went into the making of such necessary articles of furniture; for as in Homeric Greece and in Greece today chests were no doubt used for clothing, jewelry, and other valuables.

The Minoans may have had wooden chairs with backs if the gypsum throne in the Priest-King's audience chamber is, as Evans believes, a copy of a throne made originally of wood. Stools appear in the frescoes; their lines and general shape seem to indicate that they were made of wood. Since the Minoans were fond of bright colors and employed them wherever possible, they may have painted some of their wooden furniture.

Round stone-topped tables, supported on stone or wood standards with broad bases, somewhat like the marble-topped tables of the nineteenth century; lamps of all sizes, from small portable ones to great stone bowls with several wicks floating on oil; jars, large and small, all painted in gay

colors, help to form a picture of the furnishings of a prosperous household in the Golden Age of Minoan Crete.

That the frescoes represent Minoan men with deeply
tanned faces and wiry, sinewy bodies, and women with skins
that seem unusually white for people living under a southern
sun, may have been merely a convention, as it was in Egypt.
Still, the men of a household undoubtedly lived a more
active life than the women did. In the days of fresco painting
civilization on the island had advanced far beyond the stage
when the women and children spent their time hunting for
edibles. The task of food production was now in the hands of
the male, not the female. Agriculture, cattle raising, hunting,
and fishing were well established occupations for men.
Women spent more time indoors, spinning, weaving, fash-
ioning clothes—a Minoan woman's clothes were complicated
enough to take up a great deal of her time—and caring for
the numerous needs of the household.

The discovery of special seats or platforms in two houses
excavated at Knossos may possibly indicate that the head
of a family could supervise, if he wished, the life of his
household. One is the House of the Chancel Screen, so-
called because the stonework in one of the rooms resembles
that of an ecclesiastical screen; the other, which is more
elaborate, is the Royal Villa near the palace.

This villa, thought to have been the Priest-King's summer
residence, had at least two floors. An alcove with a raised
platform and near an inner light-well was so arranged that a
person seated there might overlook the occupants of both
floors and, if he chanced to be the master of the household,
satisfy himself that life moved upon a decorous plane. If he
wished to summon one of his ladies he had only to call
across to the balcony opposite him, and his desire would be
quickly gratified. The salon on the second floor had windows
with deep sills over which the ladies could lean comfortably
and amuse themselves by looking down into a pleasant little

court, where perhaps a fountain played. One wonders whether Theseus, when he forced his way into the palace, as the legend runs, may have looked up from this court and caught sight of Ariadne far above him.

Humbler folk could not have lived so luxuriously. In the outskirts of Knossos, where the excavations have shown that the bulk of the population lived, the houses of the more prosperous people had, like those of Gournia, several stories, while those of the poor had only one. Even the poorest house, however, had a small court which brought in light and air. But whatever its economic status, from the wealthiest down to the poorest, the Minoan family had become a unit, complete in itself, a secure foundation upon which to build a state.

CHAPTER TWO

FOOD AND DRINK

Although agriculture and cattle raising, probably the two most important occupations in Minoan Crete, were in the hands of men, women prepared the food for the household. They ground the grain and made it into bread. That it was a kind of hardtack is inferred chiefly from the worn teeth of a skeleton dug up one day at Knossos and brought to an eminent English physician for examination. The living flesh which once encased that bony structure, the physician decided, could only have been nourished on a hard diet. A bit of detective work—a good archaeologist must have something of the detective in his make-up—was soon set afoot to discover, if possible, what grain or grains had gone into the making of Minoan bread.

The results were disappointing. Though carbonized fragments of various grains were found in many earthen pots, positive identification could not always be made. That barley was known seems certain from numerous clay jugs with accurately molded whole ears on them. But whether barley was used to make bread as well as beer is uncertain.

The sign for cereal frequently occurs in Linear Script B, the new form of writing that was introduced into Knossos about 1450 B.C. It is impossible to decide whether this sign was intended to stand for a particular type of grain. On a seal-stone design found at Knossos a heap of grain is guarded by the royal griffin, but no one can tell whether the grain is millet, wheat, oats, or a kind of corn.

Stone hand mills for grinding grain were discovered in the House of the Sacrificed Oxen. Perhaps Homer had in mind a similar mill when he pictured the old woman who crouches over her stone in the courtyard of Odysseus's palace, resentfully grinding grain all the day long, that Penelope's suitors may have their accustomed bread.

Nothing is known about the actual process of Minoan breadmaking. The coarse flour for the suitors' bread was probably mixed with water with perhaps some melted fat added and formed into a soft dough. In Knossos the dough may have been put into baking dishes with vertical sides and projecting rims like those found during the excavation of the small House of the Fallen Blocks, in which a maker of lamps and various kinds of household utensils lived. If baking dishes or pans were not used, then the dough would have been shaped by hand into flat cakes and either baked on hot stones or buried in the hot ash and left there to bake. Both methods are used today in various parts of the world.

Nutritious though it was, since the whole grain was used, the bread itself might not suit the modern palate, for as there seem to have been no salt deposits on the island the bread is likely to have been unsalted. Whatever the process, Minoan bread was hard enough to have helped greatly in grinding down the molars of the skeleton.

Since the seeds of leguminous plants have always formed a large part of man's food, excavators are never surprised to find pots filled with remnants of beans, peas, and lentils. When the great storerooms of the Priest-King's house were opened the workmen came upon many pots filled with carbonized beans and peas. Beans like these, they told the archaeologists, often came in from Egypt, and they themselves had frequently bought them in the market. At first these ancient carbonized beans caused much excitement. Baked beans in Minoan Crete. But later, when traces of a severe conflagration were observed, this vision of succulence faded. The carbonized beans and peas were only a gruesome relic of a centuries-old disaster.

Minoan fresco painters found the trailing vetch, with its delicate flowers, admirable for artistic purposes. Its frequent use on frescoes and on vases may also mean that it was as popular a food in Minoan Crete as it was in other parts of the later Mediterranean world. Minoan painters also often represented various plants of the gourd family, such as pumpkins and squashes, all of which doubtless served as food, either cooked or raw. Boiled with meat and herbs and eaten with bread, these vegetables would be both palatable and nourishing. To dish out this ancient goulash to the members of her family some Minoan housewife may have used one of those beautifully shaped ladles now in the Candia Museum.

The excavations have yielded many perforated earthenware vessels comparable to vessels once used in other parts of the world for making cheese. Curds and cheese may, then, have been included in Minoan diet. Cheese was made from the milk of cows and goats. Cows we know the Minoans kept. Among the many so-called "cattle pieces," one shows a boy milking a cow. Goats, to judge from their frequent occurrence in Minoan art, were as numerous on the island as they are now.

In the *Odyssey* the giant Polyphemus, after milking his goats, sets aside some milk for drinking and some for cheese making. Except for this passage—and it should be remembered that Polyphemus is a barbarian—neither the *Iliad* nor the *Odyssey* mentions milk either as a food or a drink, though it is true that once in the *Iliad* a drink of wine with goat's-milk cheese grated into it is administered to a wounded warrior.

Although the legend that the infant Zeus was fed on milk and honey has been generally discredited it is interesting to-day because among the tablets found at Knossos two accompanied offerings of honeypots. In the ruins of some private houses at Knossos fragments of small earthenware pots were found, each about three inches high, some with handles, some without. Evans calls these little pots "miniature milk jugs." He thinks they may have been filled with milk to feed the family serpent. They could equally well have been pots for honey. Among the historic Greeks, milk, either alone or mixed with honey, is often mentioned but usually as an offering for the serpent member of the household.

The excavations have shown that Minoan Crete produced many varieties of fruit; quinces, plums, figs, olives, and dates are among the various fruits represented in frescoes, on coins, and among votive offerings made to deities. Of these fruits, dates seem to have been produced only in the South of Crete; at least in a southern town coins have been found representing date palms with their fruit hanging down, in process of ripening, and no such coins have been found in the colder northern part of the island. Minoan painters, however, include dates among the other fruits in their frescoes and on their vases. The models of fruits in fine-glazed clay which were found in the small shrine of the snake-goddess in the Third Palace are not so easily identified. Also among votive offerings are found shallow bowls, set on slender stems, and perhaps intended to hold fruit. It seems reasonable to conclude, then, that the Minoans must have valued fruit in their diet.

One of the numerous clay tablets discovered during the excavations aroused great interest when it was deciphered. Inscribed with Linear Script B, that ancient sign language

Gold Votive Axe (most important so far discovered);
courtesy of Museum of Fine Arts, Boston, Massachusetts;
photograph by Edward J. Moore. (Actual Size.)

North Entrance, with the Charging Bull Fresco; the Palace of Knossos; photograph by Virginia Garner.

Front View, the Charging Bull Fresco; the Palace of Knossos; photograph by Virginia Garner.

Storage Jars *in situ;* the Palace of Knossos; photograph by Virginia Garner.

Gold and Ivory Snake-Goddess; courtesy of Museum of Fine Arts, Boston, Massachusetts; photograph by Edward J. Moore. (Approximate height: 8 inches.)

The Ladies in Blue Fresco; the Palace
of Knossos; photograph by Virginia Garner.

The Procession Fresco; the Palace
of Knossos; photograph by Virginia Garner.

Pottery Vase; photograph by Virginia Garner

which had brought Evans to Crete, it contained inventories of the Priest-King's possessions. And among them was an olive grove of four hundred and five trees. Though the cultivation of the olive, which came to Crete from Egypt, is of very ancient date, until the tablet of inventories was interpreted no one knew that such a large grove had existed on the island. The export of olive oil must have formed one of the Priest-King's chief sources of wealth. Probably other large groves were set out wherever the soil was favorable to the growth of olives. Earthen jars with carbonized olives in them and others with olive pits have been found. Olive sprays appear often in the frescoes, as well as on gold pendants and other ornaments worn by Minoan ladies.

Throughout the ancient Mediterranean world olive trees and fig trees were regarded not only as valuable property but as possessing a kind of special sanctity. This was true in Minoan Crete. There the wild fig was also considered sacred, perhaps because, as has been suggested, it often grows near rocks and caverns, themselves believed to be sacred. The large pot filled with wrinkled, dried-up figs found at Hagia Triada may have contained food for the dead, but it seems reasonably certain that food offered to please the dead would have been selected because it pleased the living. It may be assumed, then, that figs formed a part of Minoan diet. And since figs are inedible before they have been ripened by artificial pollination, a method said to have been invented by the Semites, it may also be assumed that the Minoans were acquainted with that process.

The protein needs of the people were met by the eating of meat, fish, and perhaps eggs. During the excavation of some Neolithic houses on the island the bones of oxen, goats, kids, and pigs were discovered and identified. Most of these bones had been either cut or split. A large cooking pot, an axe, and some flat stones "showing traces of fire," were found nearby. This perhaps means that the early inhabitants either boiled or roasted their meat. And once people have learned to eat cooked meat they are apt to acquire a taste for it and to keep on eating it.

That meat formed a part of their staple diet may be concluded from a very interesting sign that occurs in the list of Minoan hieroglyphs. The sign has been identified as a shoulder of meat, possibly intended for sacrificial offering. The Homeric heroes always offered a portion of the sacrificed animal to the god, then roasted and ate the rest of the meat. This custom was prevalent throughout the ancient world and may well have been a custom of the Minoan world too. In Linear Script B signs for flocks and herds occur, and on seals the signs for boars and swine, also for litters of pigs. Probably pork formed as important a part of the diet of the Minoans as it does in that of a great many southern countries today.

The increasing fondness of the Minoan artist for "cattle pieces" may indicate the growing importance of meat in the diet of the islanders. Some of these pieces show recumbent cattle, a man gazing with interested eyes at a pair of oxen, another man leading a recalcitrant animal by a rope passed around its horns. Other scenes show goats being hunted by men armed with bows and spears and accompanied by dogs. Still others show men carrying home their booty, trussed and suspended from poles resting on their shoulders. After the Minoans learned to domesticate the wild goat it became a valuable animal, for it not only supplied them with meat but also with long horns to be used in making bows.

Minoan sea food included the mullet, dorado, parrot-fish, cuttle-fish, crabs, oysters, mussels, and perhaps the tunney. Piles of broken shells from the murex have been found, also numerous cockle shells, limpets, and occasionally the shell of a whelk. A large pot discovered in a storeroom contained the vertebrae of a fish. Minoan artists are fond of representing octopus, squid, and flying-fish. A seal-stone found at Knossos shows a fisherman holding up his catch, a sharp-beaked skaros, or parrot fish, and an octopus. Fish is mentioned in the *Iliad*, but the Homeric heroes seem to have looked upon fish as a food to be eaten only by those who could afford nothing better. Today in Crete fish, especially squid and octopus, is a staple diet.

Little is known about eggs as an article of diet. Probably the Minoans, like other island people, gathered the eggs of sea birds and ate them. Ostrich eggs were eaten in Egypt, where the bird was indigenous. Various Neolithic sites in the Sahara Desert have yielded thick deposits of broken ostrich eggs, but so far none have come to light from the excavations in Crete.

Some circular trays, which have aroused speculation, may possibly indicate that the Minoans raised poultry. These trays have low rims and are supported, tripod-fashion, on three short feet. Holes about the size of an ordinary hen's egg have been pierced in each tray. One tray, ten inches or so in diameter, has six holes. These trays remind one of the egg racks often used in England for serving boiled eggs. It would be interesting indeed if the Minoan trays were also intended to hold eggs.

An Egyptian medical recipe of the Sixteenth Dynasty, which corresponds roughly to the Middle Minoan Age in Crete, mentions the herbs of the *Keftiu*. In both countries herbs may have been used for seasoning food, but there is no evidence to that effect. The fragments of carbonized grain found in some earthenware pots in Knossos indicate that the islanders may have boiled their cereals. If they boiled their vegetables, too, they may have learned quite early that certain herbs would add zest to their food.

The brewing of beer and the making of wine were carried on in the island from a very early date and may even have been an industry. The inference that the brewing of beer may have been an industry is drawn from the unusual number of

jugs with ears of barley molded on them. Many of these jugs
have survived and are on display in the Candia Museum.
The making of beer in Crete is thought to have preceded that
of wine, although the cultivation of the vine was known from
prehistoric days. Intoxication was probably as rare in Minoan
Crete as it is today in Greece.

Well-to-do people in Minoan cities and towns kept their
wine presses inside their houses, perhaps for want of adequate
space outside. In the country the presses were probably outside, just as they are in rural Crete today. Apparently the
wine was not decanted, but, like the modern Sicilian wine,
contained the grape pulp. Jars have been found in the ruins
of Minoan settlements on the mainland of Greece in which
there still remained both grape seeds and lees. Since wine
making was understood throughout the whole of the ancient
Mediterranean world long before the coming of the Hellenes
it is not surprising that the word *oinos*, commonly used for
wine in historic Greece, is not really Greek at all, but pre-
Hellenic.

Wine and beer to drink, fish and meat in abundance, fruit,
green things, and various grains—certainly undernourish-
ment does not mark the people of the frescoes; and the range
of available nutriment in the days when Crete was "well
watered, fair, and fat" would seem more than adequate to
produce the vigorous people that the Minoans were.

CHAPTER THREE

THE LOINCLOTH AND THE SKIRT

Those who have formed their initial impressions of early Mediterranean dress from the statues of the Greeks and the Romans in museums or from representations in books are startled when they first see Minoan dress. They must discard all their preconceived ideas, for between classical Greek dress and Minoan dress there is no similarity whatsoever.

The Greek lady wore a flowing robe; the Minoan lady wore a low-cut bodice and a gaily colored full skirt, which makes one think of court dress at Versailles, of the farthingales worn by Queen Elizabeth I and her ladies, or of the crinolines of more recent fashion. A Minoan gentleman, with his bare torso, his striped loincloth, his necklaces, bracelets, and anklets of precious metals is a far cry from the severely clad Greek of later centuries. Why the Greeks and the Romans dressed as they did is a problem over which scholars have often puzzled. The origin of Minoan dress is more easily traced.

In prehistoric days the earliest garments worn by Minoan

men and women were fashioned from the skins of animals. The frescoes show that at first these garments were almost identical in form, consisting of an apronlike skirt that hung from the waist. Shortened, it turned into a loincloth and became the traditional costume of a Minoan man. Lengthened, it became the woman's skirt. Upon certain religious and other ceremonial occasions a long skirt reaching to the ankles was worn by both men and women. On the sarcophagus from Hagia Triada both the priestesses and the male bearers of offerings wear such long skirts. These seem to be made of panther skins, and each skirt is deeply slashed up the back and worn in such a way that one side, hanging lower than the other, slightly suggests a tail. That Minoan men wore skirts upon so solemn an occasion as that depicted on the sarcophagus—offerings are being made to a dead man—ought not to surprise anyone, since even today, as suitable dress for certain occasions, men resort to skirts, thinly disguised under the name of robes or surplices.

Although the hides of animals, with or without the retention of the tail, formed Minoan man's first clothing the great number of spindle whorls and bone needles, found even in Neolithic layers of earth, show that spinning and weaving were known in Crete from very early times. Because of its greater pliability and softness wool must soon have displaced leather as material for both loincloths and skirts. Wool could also be dyed more easily than leather, and this would appeal to the Minoans, especially to the ladies, for they loved bright-colored clothing, reds, blues, greens, and yellows.

The loincloth seems to have developed into a kind of thick truss kept in place by a tight metal belt and either padded or lined to prevent it from chafing the skin. The effect of this tight belt may have prompted the artist to portray as much as convention allowed of the broad-shouldered, narrow-hipped male form. Men therefore appear in the simplest possible garb, a gay-colored loincloth, sometimes long enough to reach to the knees, sometimes barely covering the thighs, and a belt of bronze, silver, or gold, while women are invariably represented in the most elaborate costume known to the ancient world, each sex an excellent artistic foil to the other.

The scantiness of a man's costume was more than compensated for by his silver and gold ornaments. In one of the frescoes, for example, a young man wears a high jeweled collar, broad armlets, and bracelets, all of silver. Another wears two silver armlets on the upper part of his left arm, a silver bracelet on his right wrist, and dangling from his left wrist an agate set in silver. Men of substance often wore a seal suspended from the neck, an occasional gold finger ring used as a signet, as well as bracelets and armlets. A priest-king is pictured wearing an elaborate headdress of gay-colored peacock plumes. The Minoan sphinx is decorated in the same way. Peacock plumes may have been charged with some special power or significance, but nothing is known of this. During the rainy season or the short Cretan winter men probably wore a sheepskin thrown over the shoulders or even a cloak of some kind. Chariot drivers in the frescoes occasionally wear long cloaks.

The dress of a Minoan woman was a more complicated affair. The short apronlike skirt originally worn by both sexes slowly evolved into two separate pieces of clothing, a real skirt that changed in length to suit the current fashion, and an embroidered overskirt slit part way up on either side and curved into wide scallops. One woman is shown in a short, purplish skirt, elaborately embroidered, worn over an underskirt with bright red, blue, and yellow stripes.

The earliest skirt seems to have been bell-shaped and may at times have been worn over hoops. The bell-shaped skirts to be seen in museums are the prototypes of the later fashionable crinolines. The Minoan skirt, however, never reached the proportions of the later extreme crinolines. For these in eight-eenth-century London the stairways of some fashionable houses had to be widened, and for their equivalents today school corridors are said to be proving inadequate.

Toward the close of the Middle Minoan Age the fashion in skirts changed. The bell-shaped skirt gave way to an elaborately flounced skirt that may have come in from the East, perhaps from Syria. At first rather short, reaching only about halfway to the ankle, later on it extended all the way to the ankle and sometimes below. The flounces generally began at the hips, being sewed fast to the foundation skirt just as flounces would be put on today. As the fashion changed, the number of flounces lessened, until by the six-teenth century B.C. they no longer began at the hips but near the knee. The bridal dress noted earlier—the only one of its kind on record—was flounced from shoulder to hemline. The new flounced skirt was narrower at the bottom than the bell-shaped skirt and not so easy for walking. This may have been one reason why it never entirely superseded the earlier garment.

The bridal dress is also unique in that it does not expose the wearer's bosom. Other representations of Minoan dress for women show the breasts either bared or, as some think, covered with a diaphanous chemise. In a fresco known as the Sacred Grove and Dance Fresco a group of ladies are seated in a grandstand and chatting quietly with one an-other. The ladies all wear gaily colored skirts with wide flounces and short-sleeved jackets over diaphanous chemises. Monsieur Gilliéron, *père*, who restored the fresco for Evans, has indicated the presence of the chemise by drawing a curved line at the base of the throat.

The sleeved jacket appears to have been laced up in front, somewhat like the bodice of the Swiss national costume. The sleeves were short and beautifully embroidered, much as they are today in the Balkan countries; and sometimes they were puffed. The lower part of the bodice, or jacket, was tucked into a tight belt, to which there was sometimes attached a metal framework not unlike the stiff corsets worn by our grandmothers. The marble Fitzwilliam Goddess in the Fitzwilliam Museum in Cambridge seems to wear stays made of gold strips and held in place by shoulder straps of the same metal. Some scholars think that the open bodice, with or without a chemise, was a ritual dress invented for the Minoan Goddess and later copied by the fashionable ladies. The Neolithic figurines contradict this assumption, because even at this early date the open bodice was worn by the women of the island. The transparent chemise, if worn at all, was a later addition. As for the Minoan Goddess, it is doubtful whether a ritual dress with a chemise was ever invented for her. It seems more reasonable to think that she was dressed in the current fashion. Since she was primarily a Mother Goddess nothing could have been more natural than to dress her in such a way as to emphasize her maternal function. With bared breasts she is comprehensible to all. As the human mother dresses herself, so does the immortal Goddess.

The belt or girdle that constricted the waist of a Minoan woman produced an effect strikingly similar to that seen in representations of women of fashion in the seventeenth and eighteenth centuries of our own time. That Minoan women seem to have imitated the masculine habit of wearing a tight belt is of particular interest to the twentieth century of the present era, when men's fashions are so often utilized for women.

In Crete, before the seventeenth century B.C., a woman's dress was merely a kind of cloak. Made of heavy woolen material and drawn in around the waist with a cord, the cloak would tend to bunch up around the shoulders and at the nape of the neck. In the process of being adapted to more sophisticated wear this copelike garment evolved into a dress with a high-peaked collar of the "Medici" type. Early

Minoan seals represent this dress as extending to the ankles, and the waists of the wearers appear unconstricted. The statue of the woman potter belonging to the same early period supports the information gleaned from the seals.

One special type of feminine dress is unexpected. The frescoes show young women in the bull ring apparently contesting on terms of equality with young men. The men are dressed in their customary fashion, in short, brightly colored loincloths and protective sheaths. This is what one should expect. But it is surprising to find that the young women, under these very exceptional circumstances, also wore the loincloth and the sheath.

For the most part, Minoan men and women appear in the frescoes and in other artistic representations as bareheaded. Occasionally, however, both sexes wear some kind of headgear. Two separate portraits found in the excavations show men with their heads covered. In one portrait a turbanlike arrangement is worn on the head, in the other a kind of cap. A young flute player wears a round, flat hat set well back on his head, giving him an almost feminine look. Knowledge of the hats worn by women comes almost altogether from the figurines unearthed at Petsofá, in eastern Crete. On these fashionable little ladies may be seen hats, bonnets, and toques of every description. The most interesting is a tall, horn-shaped headdress set low on the forehead and encircled by two wide stripes or bands painted upon a dark background. In spite of the difference in shape and color, there is a certain resemblance to the tall, fitted headdress once worn by Queen Nefertiti in ancient Egypt. A kind of bonnet or hood also appears, sometimes ornamented with long plumes. The snake-goddess wears a tall, pointed hat, ornamented with a coiling serpent, while her attendant votary wears a cap ornamented with the seated figure of an animal, perhaps a lioness.

The youthful flute player has short hair. So have the man

and the boy in the portraits which may be likenesses of a priest-king and his son. After the sixteenth century artists represent boxers, bull-grapplers, and other equally active men with long hair flying out over their shoulders. Sometimes the hair is twisted to form three tufts in front, with ringlets on the crown of the head or across the forehead. The manes of Minoan horses, it may be recalled, were also carefully parted and twisted into three tufts. In Homeric days men still wore their hair long. Coiled around the head beneath a helmet, it would provide excellent cushioning against a sudden blow. And everyone remembers that before the battle of Thermopylae the Persian scouts were amazed to see their Spartan enemies combing out their long hair.

Both men and women wore sandals, shoes, or boots, but apparently only out of doors. That they removed their shoes before going indoors seems likely, for the excavators at Knossos discovered that the stone steps of the inner staircases showed little trace of the kind of wear observed on the outer stairs. On the outer stairs, in spite of the slow weathering that has taken place over the centuries, faint marks of the footgear of men and women of a bygone age can still be seen. The sandals, shoes, and boots that wore away these outer stone steps were probably made of leather. They were held in place by broad straps crossing over and above the ankles, somewhat in the fashion of the modern beach sandal. The straps were often elaborately decorated with beads. Traces of paint in one fresco show that one man's boots were made of red leather and another's of white. These boots reached well above the ankles, and the legs were encased in puttees. Women may at times have worn high-heeled shoes, although perhaps only on special occasions. Perhaps Minoan ladies had a greater choice in shoes than the young bride of Xenophon's day whose bridegroom was strictly admonished to forbid her wearing high heels. Nor could she have taken refuge in the beautiful anklets of silver or of gold that were popular with both sexes in Minoan Crete. These anklets were not merely circles; they were curved to fit the contour of the ankle.

Even a cursory glance at the array of ornaments that stand upon the shelves of the Candia Museum shows how fond the Minoan ladies must have been of adorning their heads with gold or copper hairpins, their ears with rings or pendants, their throats with necklaces of filigree work or chains of beads, their arms with beautiful bracelets, or bands, made of gold or copper, and their fingers with rings set with agate, amethyst, or cornelian. A small statue of the dove-goddess wears on each wrist a bracelet set with a large gem and on each arm a string of semi-precious stones. A handsome gold bracelet discovered on Mochlos would compare favorably with the work of any European craftsman of today.

Necklaces were made by threading together beads of various kinds: amethyst, agate, cornelian, and blue paste imitations of lapis lazuli. An elegant lady from a provincial town wears two necklaces, one of gold beads festooned with loops also of gold beads and the other of blue paste. Some necklaces had three, four, or five rows of beads, often interspersed with pendants in the shape of birds, lions' heads, or flowers, especially daisies and lilies.

Pendants have been found in large numbers. Many are made of cornelian, amethyst, crystal, or chalcedony. A pendant on which Negroid figures are carved is especially fine. Beautiful gold chains, some of almost microscopic fineness, some with pendants attached, exquisitely wrought hairpins of gold, with jeweled heads, and other beautiful trinkets for the adornment of a lady's head have also come to light. Diadems of gold and of silver were probably worn not only as ornaments but for the practical purpose of confining the hair.

During the Neolithic Age in Crete, a primitive type of ornamentation was indulged in by both men and women.

This was tattooing, an almost universal custom in the early Mediterranean world. The necessary tools, needles and awls, as well as vessels containing blue and red pigments, even palettes, have been found in some of the tombs, presumably that the dead man might adorn himself in the next world as he had been accustomed to do in this one. The few examples of tattooing that have survived follow a simple pattern of one or more dots or horizontal lines, not the elaborate designs seen nowadays on the chests and arms of sailors.

The kind of clothing the Minoans wore, especially the feminine jacket and skirt, bypassed the Greek Peninsula completely, where an entirely different type of garment was in vogue for both sexes. Centuries later the jacket and skirt reappeared in Europe and has remained ever since an essential part of a woman's wardrobe. The male loincloth that hung from the waist has evolved into trousers, which still hang from the waist.

Neither the frescoes nor other artistic representations afford any information about the clothing worn by children. But one of the signs on the Phaestus Disk does seem to depict a small infant clad in a sort of loose shirt. Similar clothing can still be seen today in warm countries where a single garment is all that is needed. The chances are that in Crete an infant shirt, if worn at all was often discarded. The application of the belt at an early age may have been attended by some ceremonial observance, especially if at this time the boy assumed the loincloth of manhood, while a girl was clothed like her mother, in a short-sleeved jacket and skirt.

CHAPTER FOUR

AN ANCIENT SCHOOLROOM

In prehistoric Knossos a young Minoan, regardless of his station in life, would have had to be taught, by precept and by example, his means of livelihood. If country-bred he would learn to till the earth, raise cattle, hunt, and fish. If he belonged to the artisan class he might combine these activities with an industry or a craft handed down to him by his forefathers. Perhaps he would engage in an industry carried on in his own home, one that called for specialized training, such as stone carving, lampmaking, or the shaping of pottery. And he probably had to make most of the tools he needed for his tasks.

If he became sufficiently adept in his craft he might be summoned to the palace to join the other artisans there in manufacturing articles for the Priest-King's personal use or for export to other lands. If he belonged to the ruling class he might be taught there the principles of government and administration, the control of trade and industry, and the maintenance of proper relations between his island and the world around him.

Perhaps he received instruction in that small room in the

Third Palace which Mr. Mylonas has recently called the "oldest schoolroom in the world." The room is situated near the Queen's Suite in the east wing and not far from where the craftsmen had their workshops. Except for an opening at the rear, possibly for a door, there seems to have been no way of admitting light into the room.

Mr. Mylonas bases his interpretation of the room largely upon some of those tablets of baked clay that were found on the benches and on the floor. At the top of each tablet a sentence had been written, according to Mr. Mylonas, in "a firm and strong hand," while underneath, written in a "weaker, uncertain hand," an attempt had been made, in copybook style, to imitate the signs above. The signs were in Linear Script B. The tablets were not isolated examples of this script, for Evans discovered some 1400 of them during the first month of his excavations.

When the earth was finally removed from the room hollow depressions were seen in the pillars at either end of the stone benches against the walls. Clinging to the sides and bottom of one depression were minute particles of a substance that appeared to be a kind of ink. The writing on the tablets and the particles of ink seem conclusive evidence to Mr. Mylonas that as early as the sixteenth century B.C. "in that little room . . . perhaps were born the elements which later developed into the educational system of our western world."

But since Mr. Blegen's discovery of the Palace of Nestor at ancient Pylos it is somewhat doubtful whether the small room in the Third Palace at Knossos was used altogether as a schoolroom. For in his own palatial residence Nestor seems to have had just such a room, also equipped with a stone bench running around its three sides. Heaped on the bench and on the floor lay over six hundred clay tablets. Unfortunately, the Second World War not only interrupted the work at Pylos but caused Mr. Blegen to postpone the publication of his tablets until 1951. The world was then startled to

learn that the tablets from Pylos were written in Linear
Script B. A mystery, centuries old, was on the verge of being
solved. If only the texts could be deciphered.

Mr. Blegen thinks that the small room in Nestor's palace
may have been a storage place for the royal archives. Perhaps Minos used his room for the same purpose. The copybook tablets and the ink-like particles may have played their
part in the instruction of scribes, and great numbers of them
must have been needed in the administration of Knossos.

That the use of ink was known in Minoan Crete is clear
from some terra-cotta vases on which whole sentences have
been found, written in ink and in cursive script. On two
earthenware cups the writing seems to have been done
with a brush or with a soft reed pen dipped into dark ink or
sepia. If materials such as palm leaves or papyrus brought
in from Sicily or from Egypt ever served for writing purposes
they have long since perished.

The use of ink implies a receptacle in which to keep the
ink. A stone sphinx of Hittite workmanship, discovered at
Hagia Triada, closely resembles a Chaldean inkstand in the
form of a dog that once belonged to a king of Babylon. The
sphinx has a cup-shaped hollow in its back, similar to the
hollow cut into the dog's back. The inky black powder that
remained in the sphinx's hollow may mean that it also was
an inkpot, perhaps imported from Anatolia.

The excavations at Knossos had turned up masses of tablets,
nearly three thousand in all, in addition to quantities of incised seals and metal bars on which signs had been inscribed.
Although at the time of their discovery Evans could not
decipher their meaning he gradually learned that they fell
into an ideographic system that expressed, in crude form,
simple objects and even ideas. Then he made another discovery. Two distinct systems of writing had developed on the
island. To distinguish them from each other he called them
Linear Script A and Linear Script B. Later he found that

Linear Script A had been used throughout the island, while Linear Script B was limited to Knossos itself and might perhaps have been confined to the royal documents.

The interest of a young Englishman, Michael Ventris, whose sudden death in an automobile accident in 1956 cut short his investigations, was greatly stimulated by the publication of the Pylos tablets. During the war Ventris had become a skilled cryptographer. But when a schoolboy of thirteen he had heard Sir Arthur Evans lecture on the Minoan tablets. And the discovery of the Pylos tablets made him eager to apply his knowledge of cryptography (and of Greek) to a solution of the mystery. He was encouraged when he found that the "writing" on the tablets could be broken down into eighty-eight signs, each one apparently denoting a syllable. Some of the tablets also held minute pictures of objects: cups, bowls with two, three, and four handles. Near the bowls were signs which he took to be numbers and which corresponded roughly to the ancient Greek.

With the help of a philologist, John Chadwick of Cambridge University, Ventris gradually pieced together his clues, and in July 1952 he announced that Linear Script B, the language of the tablets from Knossos and from Pylos, was archaic Greek belonging to a period some two and a half centuries before the traditional date of the Trojan War in 1184 B.C. This unexpected conclusion has now overturned all previous theories about Greek pre-history. Scholars who accept his interpretation of the tablets believe that the Golden Age of Crete was dominated by Mycenaean Greeks from the mainland who about the middle of the fifteenth century entered into close relations with Crete, and possibly became the overlords of Knossos. Fifty years later, on a bright spring day when a strong wind was blowing, fire broke out in the House of the Double Axe and swept into oblivion all that brilliant civilization of Minoan Crete.

In 1950, Mr. H. L. Lorimer, an authority on pre-Greek

history and a member of Oxford University, had suggested that a common tongue was once spoken in Greece, Crete, Cyprus, and other islands, but that the language was not Greek. Today those who follow Ventris and Chadwick agree that it was a form of Greek, perhaps once spoken in Arcadia and carried from there to the islands.

On August 29, 1957, the New York *Times* published an article, with illustrations, on the decoding of Linear Script A by Professor Cyrus Gordon of Brandeis University. Mr. Gordon's conclusion is that Linear Script A was a Semitic language known as Akkadian and spoken by a people who once lived in the Euphrates valley. From the seventeenth to the fifteenth centuries B.C. this Semitic tongue was the language of Crete. The *Times* also reported that Mr. Gordon, using the framework set up by Ventris, had already succeeded in deciphering twelve syllables of Linear Script A. His results lead one to hope that the mystery of the Cretan tongue may soon be solved and new light thrown, possibly, on the still elusive Linear Script B.

Whether Linear Script A is a form of the Akkadian language or not and whether Linear Script B is a form of Arcadian Greek or not, the large number of tablets discovered at Knossos must mean that the islanders were sufficiently literate to make use of a written language and that this knowledge was not limited, at least during the Golden Age, to the upper classes. Perhaps the so-called schoolroom became the center from which knowledge spread.

The strongest proof that reading and writing were not limited to the upper classes or to the court circle comes from the discovery of *graffiti*, scrawled, apparently at random, on the walls of Minoan houses, obviously for the chance passer-by to read. This was also a common practice in ancient Pompeii.

Minoan writing ran from left to right, as in most modern systems. The archaic form *boustrophedon*, which means ox-turning, does not seem to have existed in prehistoric Crete.

It is derived from an ancient plowing technique. When the plowman reached the end of his first furrow he turned his beast around and started his second furrow down alongside the first. He did not waste his time and energy by returning each time to his original starting line. An inscription written in Linear Script B on a small clay object found during the excavations, although it presents its characters in the archaic arrangement, is thought to have been written by a Hittite settler in Crete. Possibly he was learning the new tongue.

In addition to reading and writing, other arts may have been taught in the schoolroom, for depressions, very useful for mixing clay, Mr. Mylonas thinks, had been carved out at set intervals in the stone benches along the walls. One can easily visualize a potter's apprentice seated on his bench, learning how to shape a vase with hands that grew daily less clumsy. Near him may have sat another apprentice learning the delicate process of stonecutting with a chisel he had made himself.

On the level directly above the schoolroom a ruined stone-cutter's shop may be seen. Traces of its occupant's handiwork still remain: a beautiful limestone amphora on which he had just put the finishing touches; another he had barely begun when catastrophe struck and the chisel fell from his hands. The finished amphora was so large that eleven men equipped with poles and ropes were needed to carry it down to the basement below. Perhaps the stonecutter had learned his trade in the schoolroom.

By the sixteenth century B.C. Knossos had prospered mightily, and schools of pottery were flourishing. And though it is impossible to say just when or where the potter's wheel was invented or when it was adopted in Crete, certainly it was already known in the Middle Minoan Age and had already created pottery in new forms and better proportions. The use of the wheel was also responsible for the remarkably beautiful pottery known, from the cave on Mount Ida where it was first discovered, as Kamares ware. This pottery is exquisite; the walls of the little eggshell cups are as thinly drawn as those of the finest Sèvres china. Such texture was never attained again by the gifted Cretan potters. And only in later Venetian glass, experts think, can equal feeling in color effects be found. It is said that the potters who produced this fine work admired the sheen which the workers in bronze had managed to attain and had finally succeeded in achieving it in their own "eggshell" pottery.

The Minoans were excellent workers in metal. They seem to have been unacquainted with the art of tempering bronze; yet with their delicate tools and dexterous hands they created things of lasting beauty. The potter's skill improved steadily after he adopted the wheel; the metalworker's skill improved in like measure when he learned that hardness could be materially increased by fire. Since the arts all have certain principles and certain objectives in view, those who practice them must inevitably learn from one another. This scholars found to be true in Minoan Crete when they compared the various artistic products of the island.

Some artists found inspiration in Egypt; others in ancient Anatolia. And all learned much from each other, passing their subjects freely from potter to bronzeworker, from vase painter to fresco painter, from sculptor to engraver. But however much they borrowed from abroad or from each other, they seem never to have lost their originality. Each art adhered to its own conventions, but each artist experimented as he pleased and created new forms. It has often been remarked that the Minoan artist's tendency toward naturalism kept him from being a slavish imitator; that though he attempted to reproduce truthfully what he saw, he looked at nature with the fresh eye of a child.

Minoan artists have been called the Japanese of the Mediterranean. However large the wall spaces that the fresco painter was expected to decorate, he tended, with some notable exceptions, to fill them with relatively small figures. In the Miniature Fresco, for example, hundreds of people were represented on a much reduced scale. In the frescoes that attempt great figures something seems lacking. The Toreador Fresco, though spirited and harmonious in composition, does not, experts have felt, show the Minoan execution at its best, nor do the more than life-size figures in the Procession Fresco, of which the Cup-bearer forms a part. Neither in frescoes nor in painted reliefs, when they present life-sized or more than life-sized objects, are the Minoan artists completely successful.

Yet the art of the miniature fresco did not last. Toward the end of the fifteenth century interest in it seems to have died away. And for the best in Minoan artistic achievement one must look at the small cult statues and at the delicate work on signet rings, seal-stones, and gems.

For about three centuries, from the seventeenth through the fifteenth, the painted relief held a prominent place. Very few specimens of this art, a combination of sculpture with painting, have been found outside of Knossos. The most remarkable example of the new technique is the beautiful relief of the Priest-King. The painting is thought to belong to the early part of the Late Minoan Age. It is executed in low relief, and it is generally admired for its knowledge of anatomy, especially that of the right forearm. The "faint muscular indications" in that part of the left arm which remains suggest to experts that the Priest-King was leading in his left hand his sacred griffin.

In contrast to the low relief of the Priest-King Fresco, the magnificent bull of Minos appears in exceptionally high relief. Visible to all who approached the House from the north, the charging bull must have filled visitors with admiration and awe. Breathing hot defiance, he challenged all comers, both animal and human. Evans calls him "one of the noblest revelations of Minoan art."

From very early days the stonecutter knew how to fashion jugs with spouts, bowls with handles, graceful vases of the soft and easily worked stone called steatite, figurines of men, women, and beasts in ivory and even in alabaster and precious metals. Terra-cotta figurines display a feeling for nature and not a little technical skill; bronze statuettes and the charming little Snake-goddess in gold and ivory show to the full the skill of the Minoan artist in these fields; but of marble no trace has been found. The island produced no marble.

The slender male figure called the Bull-leaper and the gold and ivory Snake-goddess show that the unknown artist or artists knew how to create small, lifelike statues in the round. The statue of the goddess in the Boston Museum of Fine Arts is between six and seven inches high, the Bull-leaper in the Candia Museum, between eleven and twelve. Both are rendered with a freedom and a naturalness that are exceptional, and both come from Knossos. The face of the goddess is strangely modern (Anglo-Saxon it has been called) with deep-set eyes, a technique to remain virtually unknown to the Mediterranean world for many a century.

The goddess wears a tiara, a flounced skirt, a tight-fitting jacket, and a girdle made of gold. Of gold, also, are the two lifelike serpents she holds, firmly clasped in either hand. They are considered excellent examples of the goldsmith's art. A series of holes above the forehead of the goddess may mean that a fringe of gold curls had once been attached there. The missing loincloth of the Bull-leaper may have been thin gold plating. The ivory and gold in these two statuettes is of special interest to students of later Greek sculpture, for this particular combination was brought to perfection in the great gold and ivory statues of Athene and of Zeus.

Goldwork, jewelry, stone axes, and a snake-goddess! The incongruity strikes home even more forcibly to those who study the exquisitely wrought jewelry of the sixteenth and fifteenth centuries: necklaces and pendants, gold trinkets of every shape and kind. It is said that the Minoans imported their gold from Nubia—the "Land of Gold"—the Egyptian Nub. From wherever they brought it they had enough so that they could use gold bars and rings of solid gold for currency. And gold-plating was common on bronze, on silver, and on ivory, even on the wooden horns of a bull's head *rhyton* (a libation pitcher or drinking horn). Among the finest examples of this combination of metals are the bronze daggers inlaid with gold and silver that were found in the Fourth Shaft Grave at Mycenae and that belong to the fifteenth century B.C. The gold cups from Vaphio are equally remarkable examples of the high level which the goldsmith's art had attained.

Of the training of women in such fine workmanship nothing is known. Although women seem to have lived on terms of comparative equality with men, into many fields of activity they probably did not enter. The statue of the woman potter, dating from the Early Minoan Age, may merely be that of a woman making a utensil for her own use. Yet it would be pleasant to think that if in the schoolroom boys received instruction in reading and writing, in the handling of clay, or in the making of jewelry, girls may also have benefited. And although education, or rather instruction, in commerce, government, administration, international relations, and other concerns was doubtless considered the sole prerogative of the male, one should not forget the legend that Ariadne was once left in charge of the palace and there came to terms with Theseus.

Whether reading, writing, and other special arts were taught in this room called the schoolroom is after all only an academic question, and its answer of no real consequence. What is important is that the Minoans, however or wherever they were taught, were a literate people and highly trained in the ways of their civilization.

CHAPTER FIVE

BULL-GRAPPLING AND OTHER SPORTS

Games of skill must have fascinated the Minoans. A gaming-board with a number of small cups arranged around its outer edge and with a larger cup in the center suggests the old-fashioned game of tiddly winks. A partially damaged fresco shows Minoan boys playing a similar game. But instead of a board with fixed cups, these small boys are tossing their pebbles into holes in the ground. One boy is half kneeling, supported on his left arm. He holds a pebble in his right hand, between thumb and forefinger. Near him squats a younger boy, pebble in hand, waiting his turn. And surely spectators are gathered around, showering advice as people do, or merely watching to see what luck the first player will have with his toss.

But the excavations at Knossos have clearly shown that these games played by small Minoan boys with pebbles or at times with knucklebones were only childish imitations of a much more difficult and sophisticated game that was played by their elders and, indeed, one ventures to add, by no other than the Priest-King himself. For the magnificent ivory gaming-board, or draught-board, sheltered under glass in the Candia Museum, could only have belonged to royalty. Found in a passageway of the east wing of the Third Palace not far from the Queen's Suite, it has given its name to the place where it was found—the Corridor of the Draught-board. And Evans has called it the "most magnificent relic discovered in the whole course of the excavations."

The board itself is made of small pieces of ivory joined together. Its border is of marguerites set in gold, with centers of crystal. Ivory medallions, coated with gold, mark off the part of the board that represents a fort. To win the fort seems to have been the object of the game, which was a kind of backgammon, played with dice, some think, or others think, played with flat disks resembling checkers, some of which have been found. Less elaborate gaming-boards have been found in Minoan, as in Egyptian, tombs.

The Minoans were also interested in boxing, tumbling, and wrestling. Since they seem to have demanded skill of their athletes it may be assumed that a man did not engage in sport merely to win but to display the skill he had acquired through long practice in his chosen art. Boxers were equipped with gloves and at times wore a kind of leather *cestus* wound tightly around the wrist and a part of the hand, to strengthen the muscles and keep them from being strained or torn. Minoan painters generally portrayed boxers wearing both gloves and *cestus,* as well as their customary tight metal belts.

Tumbling was an equally popular sport, and artists found in this activity good material for painting. Specialists consider their knowledge of anatomy excellent. They often showed tumblers standing on their hands or elbows, with their feet in the air. Women tumblers are sometimes portrayed with both hands and feet on the ground and the body arched backward. Since the general appearance of these tumblers stamps them as Egyptian some scholars think that Minoan women and girls did not engage in tumbling.

How popular wrestling matches were is difficult to say, for the evidence concerning them is both scanty and hard to interpret. If the Minoans, like the historic Greeks, regarded wrestling as both a science and an art, then victory alone was not sufficient; the winner was expected to win gracefully and according to the rules. Also, as in historic Greece, two styles of wrestling were probably popular: upright wrestling, in which the object was to throw one's opponent, three falls being necessary for victory; and ground wrestling, in which the struggle was continued until one of the contestants yielded.

Many other games and sports may have existed in Minoan Crete, where the incredibly blue skies and the brilliant sunshine would have brought men out from their homes to engage each other in conversation or to find companions for a game. Life was not so hard that a man, especially if he belonged to the court circle, had no leisure for participating in whatever he enjoyed most.

There is no evidence that women and girls spent much of their time out of doors or engaged in the ordinary sports of the day. But one sport, which was, indeed, more significant than a mere sport, there is evidence of their participating in. In artistic representations, at least, the young women shared in the very difficult and challenging sport of bull-grappling.

Not only was bull-grappling as exciting and as dangerous as its modern counterpart in Spain and Mexico today, but it was more difficult and more significant; for it was evidently an integral part of the Minoan religious ceremonial. The spectator of the bullfight today admires the dexterity and agility of a well-trained matador and waits, every nerve atingle, for the culmination of the performance: the killing of the bull. The Minoan spectator must have felt an even greater admiration, not unmixed with fear, for the skill of the bull-grapplers had as its objective the mastery of the bull without harming him. Although in this performance the bull was not supposed to be killed he may have been wounded. One of the scenes on the Hagia Triada sarcophagus shows a trussed bull on the sacrificial table, a dagger protruding from its neck. It is possible that the bull was wounded in the arena.

The frescoes and other representations in art show that the young bull-grapplers usually worked in pairs, a boy and girl forming a team. Their relative positions are not altogether clear. One painting shows a girl clinging to the horns of a bull; another shows her standing directly behind the bull, apparently waiting to act as a buffer for her partner, a boy who has grasped the horns of the animal, swung himself up, and is now in the act of turning a back somersault that will land him in the girl's outstretched arms.

In both Spain and Mexico the matadors have been, until recently, only men and highly trained at that. In Minoan Crete the bull-grapplers were young people of both sexes, amateurs almost, since their only training seems to have been in hunting and catching wild animals, by waiting in ambush at the end of a defile where a rope cradle had been placed. The method seems to have been to drive the bulls into the defile so that at the right moment the young hunter, lying in wait, could spring down upon his chosen animal and bring him to earth. In one of the frescoes, which may represent such an ambush, a young girl is shown in the act of hurling herself upon a bull's head.

Although Crete was not the only place in the prehistoric Mediterranean world where bull-grappling was an important part of life—it was practiced also in Cappadocia—the technique involved has never been fully understood. In spite of the evidence of the frescoes and other representations in art, some authorities hold that the entire performance was impossible; others, including Evans, feel that the evidence is too convincing to be easily ignored and that, however impossible the special physical feats represented, bull-grappling must have played a major part in Minoan life.

But bull-grappling, unlike modern bullfighting, had a more significant function than that of killing an animal in the bull ring. It was deeply rooted in Minoan religious practice. The frescoes, the vases, and the figurines tell the story. They show the bull entangled in a rope cradle; they show girls, dressed like their brothers, in loincloth and protective sheath; and they show the Mother Goddess in similar dress, as though she, too, were about to enter the royal arena and grapple with a bull. In origin, then, bull-grappling appears to have been a ritual performance in which the Goddess herself was thought to be the protagonist.

One wonders if the bull may have represented a mighty creature upon whose back the early Cretans believed their island rested. For the belief that the earth rests upon the back of a great beast is found in many early cultures. The beast is variously named; sometimes it is an elephant, sometimes a serpent or a fish. But of all the beasts named, the bull is the one most often mentioned. In primitive Moslem belief the bull is so enormous that a man must travel for two hundred years to cover the distance from one horn to the other. To travel from his head to his tail would take five hundred years. One day the bull tried to rid himself of his heavy burden by shaking his head vigorously. Just then a midge stung him in the nostril and he set up a mighty bellowing. And ever afterward the bull was known among these Moslems as "the bellower."

If, then, in prehistoric Crete men held that their island rested upon the back of a bull they may also have held that the bull with whom their Goddess or their young people in her behalf had to grapple represented the bull beneath the earth. Success in the arena would, accordingly, enhance the power and the prestige of the Goddess, who, it was hoped, could then keep the island secure against the wrath of the beast below.

Bull-grappling gave to the artists of the day excellent themes for fresco painting, for sculpture, and for many of the minor arts. Scanty and fragmentary though the evidence is, it affords a fairly convincing glimpse of an ancient contest in which human beings pitted their ingenuity against brute strength, for their own safety, as they served the Goddess whom they loved and feared.

The contests are thought to have been held in the royal arena situated near the east bastion of the palace. From here a well-preserved stone stairway, down which today scores of visitors descend, leads to a plain now overgrown but once a walled-in enclosure elliptical in form and large enough to accommodate about five hundred spectators, coming not only from the palace but also, by way of a paved road, from the town of Knossos.

Any one who has ever attended a bullfight or a *fiesta* in a Mediterranean country can easily visualize the animated scene in the ancient Minoan arena: men in blue and red loincloths, narrow-waisted and broad-shouldered, adorned with gold necklaces and anklets; women with full breasts bared to the sun, wearing voluminous, brightly colored skirts; and swarms of half naked or naked children, all crowding into the royal arena, eager and awed, awaiting the contest with the bulls.

No one knows whether an admission fee was charged. Perhaps, as in fifth-century Athens, anyone who could pay his entrance fee to the theater was expected to do so, and the state paid for the poor. The excavations have unearthed numerous pieces of bronze, each incised with vertical lines to indicate its value, and if an entrance fee was charged a bronze piece or two might have been sufficient. Once admitted, the crowd must await the appearance of the Goddess and doubtless that of the Priest-King.

The Goddess would arrive in state, dressed in full bull-grappling costume, guarded by her attendants, much as to-day at the *fiesta* when a saint or even the Virgin is displayed to the populace. In Minoan Crete a statue of the Goddess was probably brought into the arena and carefully placed in a special niche where all could see her face.

The Priest-King would also have his special place, a cano-pied throne set near the grandstand that was reserved for members of the court and other people of rank. Tall and slender, on his head iridescent peacock plumes, his bare torso aglitter with jewels, a great double axe of bronze in his right hand, a spear in his left, the Priest-King would have been an awe-inspiring sight.

The stage being set, the bulls would enter; whether one or two at a time or even more, no one may ever know, at least until the tablets are fully deciphered. Nor does any one know whether the young bull-grapplers entered with the bull against which they were to measure their skill and dexterity or whether slaves with nets or rope cradles accompanied the bull.

Though it has long been accepted that young girls partic-ipated in bull-grappling no one has explained adequately why they wore the full male costume. Scholars have ad-vanced various theories. One holds that originally the con-tests were performed by men in honor of a male deity and that when the Mother Goddess as Lady of Sports took over the games her women attendants entered the contests on equal terms with men. But this theory rests upon the assumption that in prehistoric Crete the worship of a male deity preceded that of the goddess, and for such an assump-tion no evidence has proved acceptable. Another theory, too complicated to include here, hinges upon the interchange of clothing between the sexes in early adolescence that some-times occurs in primitive societies. No theory takes into ac-count the obvious impossibility of turning somersaults on the back of a surprised bull while hampered by the voluminous skirts of a primitive crinoline age.

No discussion of Minoan bull-grappling is complete without calling attention to that carefully drawn sketch in *The Palace of Minos* which illustrates the successive bodily movements needed throughout the entire acrobatic performance. The imagination balks, however, before the difficulty involved in grasping the sharp, closely set horns of a bull, before being gored to death, and in gaining sufficient momentum to swing one's body upward. The thing seems impossible. Yet the evidence is unmistakable that bull-grappling activity which required extreme skill was one of the chief sports of a sport-loving people and that it meant to the observers and participants more than mere bullfighting, that indeed to all of them it may have meant the rededication of their lives to the service of the Mother Goddess.

CHAPTER SIX

MINOAN DANCES

Minoan dances were serious and evocative, intended to bring the dancer closer to his deity. To this end Ariadne may have danced for the Mother Goddess some morning when the dew was still wet on the grass, in her dancing place near the palace.

The river flat below the east bastion would have been an ideal situation for the dancing floor which Daedalus built for Ariadne. To reach it the Priest-King's household had only to descend a stairway and pass through a gate in the east wall. And if the Royal Villa chanced to be occupied and its household also wished to be present, a few minutes' walk along a pleasant road would have brought them there. Today this space by the river is bordered by gnarled olive trees whose ancestors may have cast their shadows across the figures moving through many a ritual dance centuries ago.

Early one summer morning in 1930, Evans stood there near an ancient olive tree, seeing with his mind's eye Minoan ladies engaged in a ritual dance. Soon he became aware of a cloud of saffron and blue butterflies, flitting through the clear air.

153

The scene put him so in mind of the dancers in one of the Minoan frescoes that he felt as though the "saffron and blue butterflies were in truth the little souls of those gay ladies." For the Minoans seem to have held the pretty belief that the souls of the dead may upon occasion return to earth in the guise of butterflies.

The fresco of which Evans was thinking is that of the Sacred Grove and Dance, now so sadly defaced that only from Monsieur Gilliéron's imaginative restoration can one gain any idea of the original. In an olive grove enclosed by a wall Gilliéron imagines men and women massed together, the men in serried rows in the background, the women in the foreground. The men in the top row wave their hands excitedly in the air. In the lower right-hand corner women in blue and saffron dresses, their long hair streaming out behind them, dance with joyous abandon and with intensity toward something unseen.

Although about five hundred spectators are gathered there in the grove to watch the dance the performers appear to be totally unaware of them. Nor are they aware of a group of elegantly dressed ladies seated in a loggia from which they have an excellent view of dancers and massed spectators alike. But these ladies are not watching closely; they chat quietly among themselves, perhaps recalling the days when they themselves danced in ecstasy in the sacred grove.

Even with the help of Gilliéron's restoration of the Sacred Grove and Dance Fresco its pattern is hard to discern. But the illustrations in less damaged frescoes, supplemented by those on vases, gems, and rings, show a great variety of patterns. Some follow a sinuous or meandering course as on the François vase, while in other patterns the dancers join hands and move in a slow, solemn fashion, much as Cretan women in rural districts still dance today. There were other forms too. A terra-cotta group found during the excavation of Palaikastro in eastern Crete perhaps illustrates a group or ring dance though the three women participants have apparently not joined hands.

Both men and women are represented as participating in dances, but no children. The women dance singly or in groups, as do the men. On the François vase young men and women dance together, tradition says, for the first time in history. The design does not indicate that they danced in couples; and yet in some parts of the world the couple dance is one of the oldest forms.

The eighteenth book of the *Iliad* describes a dance that is thought by some authorities to be Cretan in origin. Here young men and girls dance together. They dance in a great circle, each with a hand on the other's wrist; then they form in two long lines and dance alternately toward and away from each other, a type of choreography that may still be seen in Crete. A musician accompanies the dancers, playing on his lyre, while two tumblers, both young men, whirl and leap inside the circle of dancers.

According to Curt Sachs, formerly of Columbia University, whose study of the dance in various parts of the world has helped to create a better understanding of the ancient Cretan dance, all people delight in motor expression, whatever the occasion may be. Dancing, he thinks, originated in a natural physical reaction to emotional excitement. The intense concentration of the dancers in the Sacred Grove and Dance Fresco, for example, and the excitement displayed by the Dancing Lady cause him to feel that the Minoans indulged, at certain times and upon certain occasions, in a form of orgiastic or ecstatic dance in which the dancer sought to free himself from his body and enter wholly into the realm of the spirit.

The special occasions on which the Minoans danced are not always identifiable. Each occasion doubtless had its ceremonial dance, seldom permitting any variation either in step or in music, lest evil should result. A gold signet ring shows women dancing to summon the presence of their Goddess. A gem shows a man dancing to appease her before he plucks the fruit from her sacred tree. And when the grass and the flowers withered and died the Minoans may have danced in a very panic of dread, terrified lest all vegetation die and hunger spread over the land. Almost everywhere in the world the harvest season calls for a special celebration, but it is a time of rejoicing, not of fear. So the harvesters pictured on the Hagia Triada vase, scythes and sickles on their shoulders, follow closely the sistrum player, ready to celebrate with song and dance the Mother Goddess, who has so abundantly blessed them.

To recall the dancing dervishes of the Middle East today may help to clarify what Curt Sachs means by an orgiastic or ecstatic element in Minoan dancing. Those who have seen the dervishes dance know that the dancers indeed "seek to enter into the realm of the spirit." Whether the individual dervish dances alone or in a group he always follows a rigorously fixed pattern peculiar to himself; he always executes his own step and maintains throughout the whole dance his own unique physical attitude: an arm clasped over his head, bent sharply at the elbow, or held stiffly out before him at shoulder height. Gestures very like these occur in many representations of Minoan dances.

Of ecstatic possession expressed in this way the exquisite Dancing Lady is a clear example. The dancer is represented with her right arm held straight out from her shoulder and her left arm bent obliquely forward. Her left hand, its index finger extended, rests on her bosom. The flying hair of the dancer shows that the artist is portraying an ecstatic or whirl dance.

An ecstatic dancer may also be seen on one of the Vaphio gems. Unlike the Dancing Lady, who is dressed in a gay jacket and skirt, this dancer wears a skirt made from the skin of an animal. She stands on the tips of her toes, her right arm bent at the elbow and her right hand holding a flute. The left arm is raised high above her head, the hand clasping what may be another musical instrument. Her head is thrown back, her lips slightly parted, her expression rapt, as though she were seeing in a vision the divinity in whose honor she is performing her dance.

Another example of ecstatic possession occurs in the group dance shown on a gold signet ring. Here four women dance in a field of lilies. They wear long flounced skirts, and their hair streams out behind them, indicating the rapidity of the dance. The figure at the left holds her arms high, but they are bent at the elbow. The two figures at the right also hold their arms up, the palms of their hands turned toward a small flounced figure in the background, apparently suspended in mid-air. The fourth figure holds one arm down and the other up alongside her head. The small figure in the background has been identified as the Mother Goddess, who is being called from her celestial realm by the dancing women.

In the terra-cotta group from Palaikastro the three women dancers are arranged in set dance postures around a fourth woman who holds a lyre. Before the lyre player stands a dove, the bird sacred to the Mother Goddess. Evans thinks its presence means that the Goddess is incarnate in the lyre player and that the three women are engaged in an ecstatic or ritualistic dance in honor of the Goddess. The postures of the women are similar to those of the dancers in the Sacred Grove and Dance Fresco, and they cause Evans to suggest that in the fresco too the dance has as its focus the Mother Goddess, represented probably by an image.

An unusual dance, known as the Dance of the Ancient Mariners and performed on the island of Delos, is believed by some authorities to have originated in Crete. The participants were sailors who came ashore for the express purpose of averting evil from their ships. During the dance the sailors either flogged themselves or were flogged, the object being to expel the threatening evil, that good might result. At some time during the course of the dance the sailors, with hands tightly clasped behind their backs, sank their teeth into the bark of an olive tree and tore away pieces of it. Ceremonial flogging such as appears in this dance was often practiced in the ancient world, sometimes to promote fertility, both of man and beast, sometimes to assist the earth in bringing forth successfully her annual vegetation. Both ritualistic scourging and the pulling down of branches from a sacred tree, especially the olive or the fig, are believed to have been an important part of the worship of the Mother Goddess. Branches of a tree were, reasonably enough, pulled down to secure the fruit; but since to appropriate the fruit of a sacred tree is a risky thing to do, it is well to hold one's hands safely behind one's back and bite the bark of the tree to avert evil from oneself. Perhaps the sailors spat out the bark upon the ground; the gesture of spitting to rid oneself of evil was common in the ancient world and is still current today.

Of all the Minoan dances, evidence of which has survived, the most controversial—and if a recent interpretation can be credited, certainly the most spectacular—is the dance represented on the François vase. This is the *Geranos*, or crane dance, which Theseus and his companions danced on the island of Delos and which has been thought by some scholars to be in imitation of the flight of a crane. Both the meaning of the word *geranos* and the choreography of the dance have often been disputed, and various other interpretations have been offered. Dances which imitate some phase of bird life were known in Greece and may have been known in Crete.

Sachs has described at some length a dance called the Dance of the White Cranes, which was performed centuries ago in China and in which he sees some similarity to the form of the Greek *Geranos*. In China, he reports, when it was still the custom to sacrifice human beings to dead princes, there lived about five hundred years before Christ a king by the name of Hu-lu, whose daughter took her own life. Her father buried her and then built an underground passage leading to her tomb. In this passage he commanded the Dance of the White Cranes to be performed. He gathered together a group of boys and girls, enticed them with the dancers into the underground passage, and then closed the door upon them all. Sachs thinks that both the Chinese dance and the *Geranos* were round dances and that both "belonged to the cycle of vegetation rites designed to obtain rain, fertility and regeneration."

The usual interpretation of the dance illustrated on the François vase is that the artist intended to portray, in dance form, the liberation of the fourteen young Athenians from the labyrinth where the Bull-man was housed. Lyre in hand, Theseus leads his companions in a long, sinuous line around an altar of horns (is this where Sachs gets his round dance?), while Ariadne stands nearby, holding aloft a ball or, as some say, a strand of wool.

Some years ago Professor Lillian Lawler of Hunter College offered a new interpretation of this dance of Theseus and his companions on the island of Delos. According to Miss Lawler, the word *geranos* is derived from an Indo-European root meaning to "wind." The dance belongs to a type of maze dance that imitated the sinuous movement of a serpent and that was performed in honor of a female chthonian, or underworld, divinity. In Crete, where Miss Lawler thinks the dance originated, the divinity may have been represented by a great serpent, possibly a python. She suggests, therefore, that since the legendary number of the Athenian captives was fourteen and since fourteen people are about the right number to dance while carrying a python skin, fourteen people may have danced the *Geranos* dance, both in Crete and on the island of Delos. Miss Lawler thinks that the dance was performed at night, around a horned altar, and that its purpose was to invoke the presence of the Mother Goddess. At the close of the dance there may have been exhibited to the dancers and to the spectators a live python, the Goddess incarnate. Miss Lawler does not suggest that in Crete the Athenian captives were the dancers, but she does think that perhaps, when the dance ended, the captives may also have been shown a living python, the visible symbol of the great Goddess herself.

If this rather startling interpretation is correct the *Geranos* dance must have been the most spectacular and the most terrifying of all ancient Minoan dances. But perhaps it is less typical than those dances that evoke the beneficence of the Mother Goddess with less terror.

CHAPTER SEVEN

RITUAL HORNS

Religious practices were, it is already evident, deeply rooted in the life of the Minoan people. Their worship was ritualistic, its focus a goddess who symbolized for them not only the bountiful, all-giving earth but also every aspect of nature. Although, like other early peoples, they had no conception of the function of the blood stream, they doubtless soon learned that if an animal or a human being loses enough blood he dies. For this, if for no other reason, blood offerings formed an important part of their religious practice.

The Minoans had no priests, as the term is understood today; the Priest-King combined in himself the functions of both king and priest. He stood in a special relationship to the Mother Goddess. His House was her shrine and she its protector. The houses of private citizens also had their shrines. Wealthy people had chapels in their houses, equipped with libation tables, precious vases, and cult vessels of gold or silver, often in the shape of a bull's head. Poor people probably set aside a corner in which to keep their humbler vessels. Here they would bring their offerings: a flower or two, a bit of fruit, and whatever else they could spare.

Each of the three important features of Minoan religion—ritual horns, or horns of consecration; the double axe; and the pillar—was the object of cult, and each was identified in its own way with the Mother Goddess. Horns decorated her shrines; miniature double axes were set up in her places of worship; pillars and trees were considered her favorite places of abode. Of almost equal importance in Minoan religion were also two living creatures: the serpent, a creature of the earth, and the dove, a creature of the air.

Today when the visitor to Knossos approaches the palace of Minos one of the first things he sees is a pair of colossal white horns. Framed in the distance beyond the horns rises Mount Juktas, with the fabled profile of the Cretan Zeus outlined against the blue sky. The white horns stand on the roof of the restored west wing of the south propylaeum of the palace. Perhaps more than anything else the sight of these great horns makes the visitor sharply aware that he is actually looking at what was once the famed residence of the priest-kings of Minoan Crete, more than thirty-five hundred years ago.

The west wing is an appropriate place on which to mount a pair of horns, not only because the horns themselves provide a noble setting for the holy mountain where the god sleeps his eternal sleep, but because they serve to mark the position of the magnificent porch through which the Priest-King's visitors once entered the House of the Double Axe. The horns were brought here from a place just north of the east hall, where they were found, and set up on the west wing because the excavators thought they might have formed, originally, part of a monumental structure intended as a place of worship. Originally, too, a huge double axe may once have rested between the colossal horns.

Of lesser dimensions and fashioned of other materials, horns of similar shape appear everywhere on the island. Stylized, they form the coping of many a building; in miniature they surmount altars and shrines; and magnified they serve often as bases for double axes. They are painted on pottery; they occur in frescoes and on seals and gems; and they may even have been worn as prophylactic amulets. They are not peculiar to Crete. But although they have been found in Majorca, in Malta, and in other Mediterranean countries, they play a more significant part in Minoan religious practice than they play elsewhere.

Ritual horns do not appear in Minoan art or architecture before the Middle Minoan Age, approximately 2200–1800 B.C. On Mochlos, however, where important discoveries have been made, a pair of rudely formed horns of red clay was found and identified as possibly belonging to the Neolithic or Early Stone Age. These clay horns are, as yet, the earliest on record. Some experts think that they may well be the precursors of the later ritual horns.

During the centuries that followed the Middle Minoan Age the use of ritual horns increased steadily. A crystal gem found in a cave on Mount Ida shows an altar with incurving sides and surmounted by a pair of horns. Trees grow in the background. To the left of the altar a female figure stands, a conch shell raised to her lips. The cave also contained fragments of terra-cotta conch shells painted red and white. Similar shells have been found in other small sanctuaries on the island. The female figure may be an attendant who is summoning the deity. Or perhaps she is calling the people to worship.

An unusual design was discovered by Hogarth on a bronze tablet from Psychro Cave. It was composed of three ritual horns, with various other objects grouped around them. These objects were easily identified as trees, birds, the sun and the moon, a fish, and a dancing male figure with his name inscribed beside him (no doubt so that his deity would be sure to recognize him). One of the birds, a ringdove or wood pigeon, is seated on the topmost branch of a tree, which bends low beneath its weight. In this rather naïve fashion the artist tells the spectator that the deity has arrived and is now incarnate in the person of the dove.

The tablet belongs to the Middle Minoan Age. The significance of the horns in the design seems to lie in the number three. The dove has been interpreted as a symbol of the Mother Goddess, who, in the shape of one of her familiar creatures, has manifested herself to her dancing worshiper. The special significance of the three other objects is easily understood; they symbolize the vast extent of her realm, since earth, sea, and sky all belong to the Mother Goddess. To make the matter even clearer, the artist has added the sun and the moon.

A triple libation table of black steatite was also found by Hogarth in Psychro Cave. It was lying on the original floor of the cave, about six meters down, under a heterogenous pile of bones of animals, broken pottery, the blade of a double axe, and the horn of a wild goat. The discovery of this libation table with its three hollows into which offerings could be poured and the discovery of the bronze tablet with its triple horns led Evans and Hogarth to conclude that in Psychro Cave underworld rites were performed to propitiate the dead. Similar rites were once performed in Arcadia, where a threefold libation was poured "first with honey, next with sweet wine, lastly with water."

The excavations at Knossos have shown that there existed in the House of the Double Axe, from the time of its first building until its final destruction at the beginning of the fourteenth century, a small shrine scarcely larger than a cell in which two pairs of ritual horns formed a part of the sacred furniture. The horns stood on what Evans describes as a "raised base of clay and rubble with a plaster facing that ran from wall to wall." Each pair of horns—neither pair was more than a few inches in height—contained a socket. In the debris on the pebbled floor lay a miniature double axe with a shaft that fitted easily into the socket of the horns. Although further search failed to produce a second miniature axe, today the small sanctuary is called the Shrine of the Double Axes.

Stylized horns formed the coping of the House of the Double Axe. In the Miniature Frescoes they form the low parapets. They seem to have rendered sacred any building to which they were attached. Part of the proof that the large building at the port of Nirou Khani served a religious purpose comes from the discovery there of a great pair of horns. Though the horns were in fragments it was clear that they had stood on a kind of dais in a paved court around which the building had been constructed.

Remains of a gigantic pair of ritual horns were found in the east hall of the Third Palace, where it is thought that a nine-foot statue of the Mother Goddess once stood. These horns, now in the Candia Museum, may have been placed on the floor before the statue. The presence of the horns, added to other evidence, justifies one in feeling that the east hall had many of the characteristics of an ancient temple.

A pair of ritual horns may have accompanied a Minoan when he was laid to rest in his tomb. Such horns were found in many tombs. In the magnificent Temple Tomb—so named because a small temple had been built above the vault—a pair of horns was discovered, not in the sepulchral chamber, but standing on the floor of the temple, to which the family and friends of the dead person had direct access by means of an open-air roof terrace.

The Benaki Museum in Athens contains a gem with an intaglio design in which a pair of ritual horns determines the divine character of the central figure, a young male, nude except for his loincloth, at whose feet the horns lie. A winged goat rears up to look into the eyes of the youthful figure. Behind him and a little to the right a half-human creature holds between his forepaws a small pitcher and is about to pour a libation to the young god, presumably of blood. Blood offerings were made to ritual horns, to double-bladed axes, and to pillars, all associated with the Mother Goddess. Although both the bull and the goat are portrayed in sacrificial scenes, where blood is being drawn, the bull appears more often than the goat. And the ritual horns so prominent in Minoan religion are never the horns of the goat but always of the bull.

In Plato's description of the sacrifice of a bull on the mythical island of Atlantis, the bull was led to a pillar, or column, on which the law and a curse were engraved. Here he was slain and his blood "brought into contact" with the pillar. This sacrifice has been variously interpreted. For example, Jane Harrison, late of Newnham College, Cambridge, England, whose theories have always attracted attention, feels that it is the life of the bull, his *mana*, that is being sought and that the pillar represents a tree, presumably a fruit tree. She finds confirmation of her belief in the sacrificial scene painted on the sarcophagus from Hagia Triada, the date of which has been set between 1500 and 1300 B.C.

The sarcophagus, also in the Candia Museum, shows the actual sacrifice of a bull. Securely bound, the animal lies on a table, the blood from his gashed neck dripping into a vessel below. Under the table two goats await their turn. Nearby stands a male votary, holding aloft in his hands the small figure of a bull. A male flute player, followed by three women in long robes, approaches the table. Here another woman waits patiently. When the vessel into which the blood drips is full, it is emptied into a two-handled vessel that rests between two pillars. The pillars are surmounted by double axes and by birds that look like doves. At the right stands a small shrine, topped by a pair of ritual horns.

In this scene the artist has included the ritual horns, the double axe, and the pillar, all closely connected with the sacrifice of a bull to the Mother Goddess. For that she is present at the sacrifice is clearly evident from the birds seated on the pillars. The sacrifice completed, the horns will be set upon an altar or in a conspicuous place, that offerings may be brought to them, possibly to appease the spirit of the dead creature or to summon the Goddess to take possession of them. Charged with divine afflatus because of their contact with deity, they will have become insurance against future disaster.

CHAPTER EIGHT

THE DOUBLE AXE

The double axe was as significant and as important in Minoan religious practice as the other two objects of cult, the ritual horn and the pillar. Although the pillar has survived in the tombstone, and the horn has survived in the numerous representations of a bull's head with its great, sprouting horns, the symbol of the Minoan Age in Greek history is neither a pair of horns nor a pillar; it is, throughout the whole of Greece and especially in Crete, a double-bladed axe.

Tradition knows that Hephaestus once used a double-bladed axe to open the head of his father Zeus. And no sooner had Hephaestus complied with his father's request than out sprang the goddess Athene. The myth occurs frequently in Greek literature and seldom without mention of the double axe.

A familiar scene in the *Odyssey* shows Odysseus performing a remarkable feat. Pretending to test Penelope's suitors, he set up at the far end of his hall twelve axes in single file. Then he challenged the suitors to try their strength, one by one, upon his own bow, which he had left behind when he went off to Troy. After they had all failed to bend the bow he caught it up, bent it, and sent his arrow straight through the twelve axes.

Before Knossos was discovered this exploit was dismissed as an impossible poetic exaggeration. Now the excavations have uncovered huge bronze axes with flaring, crescent-shaped blades and with holes in the center of the heads which make one reconsider that judgment. These axes resemble medieval battle-axes or broadaxes, except that they have two blades instead of one. Set on tall standards and ranged against the wall of one of the rooms of the Candia Museum, these axes by their special shape and by their immense size— one measures about forty-five inches in width—at once attract the visitor's attention.

The origin of double-bladed axes must be sought in the single-bladed axe of the Neolithic or New Stone Age, the earliest stratum on the island which has as yet yielded any finds. Although the only examples of a single-bladed axe that have been found are miniature in size, each one, like the big axes, has a hole in the center of the head for the handle to pass through, unlike the modern axe, in which the head is inserted into a slit in the handle. One of these miniature axes is made of black steatite, with a perforation at the end of the handle, which perhaps means that it was to be worn as an amulet.

To transform his single-bladed axe into a double-bladed axe a Neolithic or Early Minoan man had only to trim away the blunt side of his axe head until he had made two thin flanges or wings, retaining the hole of the center of his axe head for the insertion of the handle. If the poet of the *Odyssey* had in mind double-bladed axes with such holes in the center of the heads a good marksman like Odysseus might have sent an arrow through twelve axes set up in a row, one behind the other.

The earliest examples of the double-bladed axe as yet dis-

covered in Crete belong to about the middle of the Early
Minoan Age. One is a small copper axe from a tomb on
Mochlos. Miniature double-bladed axes, each with a perforation at the end of its handle like that in the single-bladed
Neolithic axe, have also been found. Since they are too large
to be worn as amulets, they may have been intended for
votive offerings, to be suspended from a shrine or from the
wall of a tomb. To suspend objects in this way was a common
practice in antiquity and is not unknown today.

A strange type of double-bladed axe appears on the Hagia
Triada sarcophagus and occasionally on seal-stones and in
frescoes. The blades of these axes have double edges, which
surely render them unfit for practical use. Also the blades
are sometimes decorated with what appear to be ribbons or
with festoons of beads. Many scholars believe that they are
ritual axes, dedicated, like the ritual horns, to the service of
the Mother Goddess, a reasonable inference from their frequent appearance in representations of shrines sacred to her.

During the course of the excavations at Knossos the archaeologists observed that the west wing of the palace, where
the Priest-King had his official quarters, contained an unusual number of double-axe symbols. They were incised not
only upon the stone building blocks but also upon the stone
pillars in the underground crypts. And small stone axes also
stood upon the altar of many a shrine. Someone suggested
that the sign of the double axe was merely a mason's mark,
but this interpretation found few adherents. Most scholars
continued to feel that the unusual number of double-axe signs
in the west wing emphasizes the earlier conclusion that a
special sanctity was attached to this wing of the Priest-King's
palace.

It is not clear whether the sanctity of the west wing sprang
from its use as the Priest-King's treasure room or that his
treasure was placed here because of the sanctity already attached to the wing. A Greek temple served a twofold purpose.

It was, first of all, the home of the god. But in its rear chamber the priests stored the temple treasure, for surely the god would protect his own. The west wing of the Third Palace may have been regarded in the same way, primarily as a sanctuary.

Although the east wing also had many symbols of the double axe, so many, in fact, that the two lower floors are known as the Lower and Upper Halls of the Double Axes and although the wind served certain religious purposes, as in the east hall, where the Priest-King had caused his workers in gold and ivory to erect a noble statue of the Mother Goddess, the wing itself could not have been called a sanctuary.

The lower hall, which was in a better state of preservation than the upper one, at once created the impression that it was intended for a royal reception room. It was decorated with a band of painted spirals above the dado and with large shields shaped like a figure eight and so painted as to appear suspended from pegs driven into the spiral band. The conjecture that this hall was a royal reception room was supported by the discovery of the gilded fragments of the wooden throne with a place for a canopy and by the position of the crooked passageway between the Queen's Suite and the hall which insured that no one entering from this corridor would pass in front of the throne.

The belief that the east wing had a limited religious character even though it could not be called a sanctuary like the west wing sprang not only from the many signs of the double axe incised on the pillars of the lower hall but also from the discovery elsewhere in the wing of ritual vessels and other sacred utensils. In the Queen's Suite was a stand for a double axe, serving perhaps as a shrine. Other sacred objects were found in special rooms. And the east hall itself may have been used as a gathering place for those who brought their offerings to lay at the feet of the Mother Goddess.

The sacrificial scene on the sarcophagus from Hagia Triada

shows two tall shafts, or pillars, each surmounted by a double axe and a bird, a small building with a parapet of horns, and a sacred enclosure surrounded by trees that resemble pillars. The other scene shows a trussed bull lying on its back on a table and a priestess pouring the blood from the bull's throat into a vessel that stands between two roughly shaped pillars or tree trunks. The priestess wears the slit skirt customary upon such occasions. Behind her stands a companion, wearing a robe that falls to her ankles and on her head a crown adorned with sphinxes. The two vessels she carries, suspended from a pole resting on her shoulders, have the same coloring and shape as the vessel from which the priestess is pouring the bull's blood.

The presence of the winged creatures perched upon the axes has been interpreted to mean that through the libations of blood from the sacrificed animal the deity is being summoned to take possession of the instruments of sacrifice, accept the blood offering, and grant permission to the dead man to return for a time to the world of the living. It seems likely that the instruments of sacrifice are the axes shown here on top of the pillars; but they may be the symbols of the actual instruments. If the deity takes possession of them, they will then become charged with spiritual force. Music must have formed a part of this ritual, for on the sarcophagus there are two musicians, one of whom plays the double pipe, the other the lyre, perhaps to "charm" the deity into descending from the upper air and accepting the offering of blood. And surely Evans is right in calling the deity the Lady of the Double Axe.

This Lady of the Double Axe must be the Mother Goddess herself, capable of appearing to her worshipers in various forms, as a bird or a serpent or even as an axe. The modern mind finds this difficult to understand, but to the Minoan or to the later Greek it was easy enough. Deity, spiritual force, *mana*, call it by whatever name we will, was immanent in all things, animate or inanimate. All things, then, were upon occasion objects of fear and respect, and they must be propitiated, otherwise no man knew how he could continue to live. The Lady, too, must be propitiated. The blood of the bull, shed for her, would cause her to descend from on high and enter the double axe, her alter ego.

Historians say that prehistoric Crete passed through the Aniconic Age, as other early peoples seem to have done. The term refers to a period in the history of world culture when material objects—a spear, a rock, a tool, a man's hunting-knife, or his rude stone axe—appeared to him to be a power external to himself. When he is out hunting, his spear or his axe, to his great surprise, often brings down an animal, apparently without help from him. Upon other occasions when he has tried to do this thing he has not succeeded. Now after repeated successes he begins to think of his weapon as an extension of himself, a kind of third arm. He will respect his weapon, perhaps even make offerings to it, hoping that its strange ability to slay the animal that is either dangerous to himself or that will provide him with food and clothing will pass into his own arm and body and charge him with its own peculiar virtue.

In some such fashion as this the worship of a stone axe in early Crete may have originated. An axe that can stop the ferocious, thundering approach of a wild bull is indeed worthy of respect. But the axe itself becomes an object of fear also, for it has killed the beast and the beast may be enraged at losing his life and demand satisfaction in blood. If he does not gain satisfaction his brother may send forth those fearful bellowings from beneath the earth. Or he may enter into the body of another brother on earth and gore to death the young men and women who, in honor of the Goddess, confront him in the royal arena. However the cult came about, and scholars can only grope blindly for its root, it was early established on the island and died out only after the Age of Palaces had passed away.

Although some evidence indicates that a cult of the double axe existed in Egypt at a very early date, none indicates that the cult came from Egypt to Crete. Its origin is to be sought elsewhere, and Lydia seems to have the best claim. According to a widely accepted theory, the key to the mystery lies in the interpretation of the Lydian word *labrys*. This theory holds that *labrys* means double axe and that *labyrinthos* was actually the place of the sacred axe. Tradition made it the place of the Minotaur. Protected by the horns of the bull, by the double axes, and by the other sacred emblems, the *labyrinthos,* or palace of the Priest-King, especially the west wing with its many pillared shrines and underground crypts, became a fortress against which men hoped the powers of evil might not prevail.

Wherever the Priest-King looked he could see the sacred *labrys,* incised on the walls and pillars of his House or cut from bronze and set on tall bases of variegated stone, the flat, curved blades projecting far beyond the base. At all times the double axe was a reminder that he held his supreme authority only by the favor of his divine Lady, the Mother Goddess, to whose service the Cretan *labrys* was dedicated. And as he accumulated treasure surely he could store it in no better place than in his divinely protected house.

The cult of the double axe was not confined to the palace. When the Priest-King's other residences were discovered and excavated special rooms were found (as in many private houses, too) which seemed from their contents to have been set aside for definite religious purposes. Some were apparently dedicated to the family serpent; others, to the cult of the horns; still others, to the double axe.

The small Shrine of the Double Axes was discovered in 1902. Although it dates from a late period of palace architecture it stands where an earlier shrine had stood for a long

time, and it had had, apparently, a continuous history. The
theory that axes may have been originally inserted into the
sockets of the ritual horns on the shelf is partly borne out by
one of the panels on a sarcophagus found at Palaikastro, not
far from Knossos. On this panel a slender column serves as a
base for a pair of horns, and between them rises a double axe.

The ritual axe now rests upon the horns, symbols, both of
them, of the sacrifice of the bull, whose male force has been
released, perhaps to propitiate the Beast who bellows or the
Lady of the Underworld, who is also the Mother Goddess,
perhaps to fructify the earth so that she will once more send
up the green shoots upon which man depends for his daily
food.

As the representative on earth of the Mother Goddess, the
Priest-King may be permitted to wield the sacred double axe.
With its aid he may even slay the bull, but he must be careful
afterward to thrust the weapon into its proper place, between
the horns of a symbolic bull. If he fails in his ritual duty the
blood of the slain bull may not be acceptable to the Goddess.
But if he carries out his priestly function well, after death his
body may rest in peace. And he himself may dwell forever in
the After World with his Mother, whom he has so faithfully
served.

CHAPTER NINE

THE PILLAR

Although the double axe remains today a symbol of the ancient Minoan civilization ritual horns long ago lost their significance. And the third of Nilsson's objects of cult, the pillar, which once played an equally important part in Minoan thought, custom, and religion, had been long forgotten until the excavations restored it to the trinity of symbols to which the Minoans attached their fears and their faith.

While a small room in the Third Palace was being cleared a miniature shrine of painted terra cotta came to light. The shrine is composed of three stubby columns set on a common base but with no common entablature. Each column is topped by a square block or capital, above which project the roof beams of a building. And upon each beam a dove perches. A somewhat similar arrangement of triple columns occurs in the Temple Fresco. Parallels also exist in many Semitic cults. The absence of a common entablature above the three columns of the miniature shrine has caused much dissension among scholars. Evans believes that the doves symbolize the presence of the Mother Goddess and that the Minoans worshiped each column as a separate religious entity. Other scholars concede that the doves symbolize the Goddess, but they see no significance in the absence of a common entablature and prefer to regard the three separate columns as a mere architectural device.

The disagreement hinges on the purpose served by a column or a pillar, especially in an underground crypt. Is the pillar merely functional? Or has it also, in certain places and under certain conditions, religious meaning? If it is a holy object is it holy in itself, or does it acquire sanctity through religious usage? In other words, is the pillar a relic of the Aniconic Age and does it belong in the category of baetyls, stones such as meteorites or others of peculiar shapes, which are considered sacred in themselves because they are thought to be the dwelling places of holy spirits?

Underground crypts with pillars have been found not only in the Third Palace at Knossos but also in the palace at Phaestus and in other buildings, notably in the eastern part of the island, where earthquakes are frequent. In the center of a crypt in the palace at Knossos stand two square pillars. Each is incised with the sign of the double axe, and each is hewn from a single block of stone.

Such pillars as these, which are among the earliest examples of the use of monolithic pillars in crypts, were later replaced by columns made of separate blocks of stone neatly fitted together. The striking thing about these particular pillars is that they, like many others discovered in crypts, were more massive than they needed to be as structural supports. Scholars have often pointed this out. They have also pointed out that some of the underground pillars, whether monolithic or not, were obviously not even intended for support, since their tops do not reach to the ceiling. Occasionally pillars stand on thin slabs of stone that project on all four sides. In the miniature shrine found at Knossos all three columns stand on a common base, perhaps representing the floor of a crypt. That blood sacrifices were performed in these crypts is indicated not only by the discovery of the remains of several skulls of urus bulls but of narrow channels in the floors that lead into shallow vats. Such channels and vats have been found in more than one crypt.

Most pillars in underground crypts are incised with the sign of the double axe. But some are also marked with the sign of the trident: the insignia of the god Poseidon, with whom the Greeks often associated the bull. Of two pillars in one crypt of the Third Palace, each composed of four blocks, one has the double axe cut into three consecutive faces; and both have it on the horizontal face of the upper block. The sign of the double axe is also carved on the stalagmites, or natural pillars, of Psychro Cave.

The sacrificial scene on the sarcophagus from Hagia Triada also shows pillars associated with the double axe. The pillars resemble trees, and the trees in the sacred enclosure resemble pillars. The priestess pours the blood into a vessel that stands between the pillars, or trees. And it has been suggested that her next act will be to empty the blood from the ritual vessel at the foot of one or both of the pillars. Scholars have long sought the origin of this strange custom of pouring a blood offering before a pillar. Perhaps the most plausible explanation as yet offered is that the origin of the cult is twofold, the veneration paid in ancient times to stones, especially that paid to standing stones, and the veneration paid to trees.

On the island of Malta there existed in prehistoric days an elaborately organized cult with pillars as the chief object of worship. The priests attached to the cult had mysterious ways of communicating with the worshipers. And in both Crete and Malta the pillar cult was associated with the worship of "matronly divinities." Some scholars hold that its origin is to be sought in the baetylic stage of primitive religion and that the pillar had become to the Minoans the dwelling place of a spirit and consequently possessed a sanctity of its own. Other scholars dispute this view. They believe that a pillar cult existed in prehistoric Crete as in Malta but that the sanctity of the pillar cannot be traced to a baetylic source. Sanctity, they hold, is not inherent in the pillar; it is communicated to it from an external source, from a blood offering, from the presence of a winged creature perched upon its summit, or from the widespread early custom of marking with a stone the final resting place of a dead person.

At this point a brief digression may be in order. Amarnath Cave in the Himalayas contains a pillar of solid ice that for centuries has shown no signs of melting. The pillar, or *linga,* as the Hindus call it, is the symbol of Siva, the god who with his wife Parvati once lived in the cave and still does, according to some of his worshipers. In Hindu belief Siva has the power to remove man from the earth and to confer immortality upon all who make a yearly pilgrimage to his cave. And each year thousands undertake the long, hard journey. Each brings an offering—food, clothing, whatever he can—to place before the *linga.* Although many pilgrims perish along the way countless numbers reach the cave and gain the blessing of Siva, immortality.

In the Middle Minoan Age the tombstone of a man may have been regarded as the earthly tenement of his spirit. If he chanced to be absent at any time, he might be induced to return, provided that ceremonies both appropriate and pleasing were performed. The next step in cult observance would be the erection of a pillar shrine as the abode of the divinity in whose charge the departed spirit was. And the pillar, or column, would always remain an object of veneration.

The divinity could have been no other than the Mother Goddess. She is often shown seated upon a pillar or upon a rocky peak behind which there can be seen a pillar shrine. Here she receives her offerings: the fruits of the earth, the products of the sea, or the warm blood of a bull. Probably the worshipers were not clear in their own minds whether they were adoring the Mother or the pillar, or whether, as is more than likely, the two had become one and the same.

Like other early peoples, the Minoans worshiped trees. The two pillars in the sacrificial scene on the sarcophagus from Hagia Triada, into the tops of which double axes are thrust, look more like the trunks of trees than like square-cut pillars. They might almost be palm trees from which the fronds have been hacked off. In the other scene birds perch on the tree-like pillars, just as they do on the three columns of the miniature shrine of terra cotta. Since in early Minoan belief the presence of a winged creature signifies possession by a deity the tree upon which a bird alights must be thought of as consecrated to the service of deity, here to the Mother Goddess in another of her many manifestations, that of a tree-goddess.

In Minoan art sacred trees are generally surrounded by a protecting wall. Sometimes, as in the scene on the sarcophagus, a building stands nearby. Or there may be an altar or a small shrine near a tree or a grove of trees. Nilsson distinguishes between these two types of artistic representation. A protecting wall, he thinks, indicates a rustic cult; a shrine or altar, an urban cult. He also thinks that the cult itself belongs originally to the countryside. A scene in which people are shown dancing before a tree he interprets as an entreaty to the spirit of the tree, the tree-goddess, to appear and accept the offerings of her votaries.

Since a tree or a plant is instinct with that life which is common to us all it is not surprising to find that among the Minoans, who, like other early peoples, passed through the animistic stage in which all natural objects are infused with spirit, a tree should be regarded as the abode of deity. Nor should it be surprising to find that ecstatic dancing formed a part of the adoration of a tree. It is noteworthy, however, that almost always the tree before which the votaries dance is a fruit-bearing tree and that the dancer is represented as grasping or touching the tree, possibly to pluck the fruit and present it to the Goddess. This ritual drama is, in one representation, performed by a naked priestess or attendant who, dancing with orgiastic abandon, shakes down the fruit from the tree.

The Minoans revered not only the olive tree and the fig tree; they also revered other trees, especially palms. The date palm is not considered indigenous to Crete; it was probably brought in by the Minoans at an early period, for it was already familiar enough in the Middle Minoan Age for the fresco painter to make use of it. Palm groves appear on seals and sealings. The palm leaf lent itself well to the hand of an artist. Now and then palms appear on signet rings. That olive trees, fig trees, and date palms should be protected and even regarded as sacred is understandable enough; their fruits provide a large part of man's food. But the same reasoning cannot be applied to the pine, the cypress, and the plane. Perhaps as in other instances necessity played its part, for as the overseas commerce of the island increased, wood was needed for building ships lest the Priest-King's maritime trade languish and die.

Some scholars think that the association with religion of the lily, the sacred flower of Crete, comes from the fact that the ancient cult of the tree spread to certain flowers, to young plants and to shrubs, perhaps only to those that were rare and hard to grow. Also, some things pass quickly away and may not come again. So man must revere them, must dance and stamp with his feet upon his great Mother, the Earth, to assist her in her struggle to bring them back.

The return of the vegetation might be hastened, the people of historic Greece once believed, by the performance of a curious rite that was practiced in their country up to a very late date. The rite is known to folklorists as the Swinging Cult. In Attica, that part of Greece where only women and girls practiced the rite, swinging formed a part of the *Aiora*, the feast which celebrated the ripening of the grapes. Elsewhere the purpose seems to have been to assist the earth in producing her vegetation. To achieve this end hostile spirits must be driven away and friendly ones persuaded to come in their place.

Our only knowledge of the possible existence of the cult in early Crete comes from a miniature terra-cotta swing in the Candia Museum. The group was not found as a whole but in fragments that could easily be put together. The swing is suspended between two upright supports, or pillars, each of which is surmounted by a dove. The small female figure seated in the swing is thought to represent either the Mother Goddess or one of her attendants. Some have interpreted the terra-cotta swing as a reproduction, in miniature, of a child's swing. The presence of the doves on the upright supports should preclude this interpretation. Unfortunately, an exact interpretation of the swing with its entrancing little figure is impossible, since it is the only one of its kind.

Whatever the origin of the cult of the pillar it played a notable part in Minoan religion. The Little Palace is a good illustration, for since underground pillar crypts occupied about a fourth of its total area they must have been built to serve as places of propitiation. Appeased, even fed, by the blood of a bull poured at the foot of a pillar, the powers below might be willing to hold the earth steady beneath the feet of man.

The standing stone, or pillar, and the sacred tree are both associated with deity, and the Lady of the Pillar and the Lady of the Tree are but manifestations of that matronly Goddess whom the Minoans adored. The three are one and the same. They spell unity rather than trinity, that underlying unity which is the source of all things and in which all things merge. Offerings made to one are offerings made to all. If propitiated by appropriate sacrifice and ritual they will allow the vegetation to return, and the dead man to live again, and perhaps they will even ward off the wrath that comes from below. The Mother Goddess is the stabilizer of the earth. Endowed with her divine power, the stabilizing pillar, if man does his part, will hold the earth secure.

CHAPTER TEN

THE SERPENT AND THE DOVE

Creatures which, without feet or wings, can suddenly and mysteriously disappear from sight, and other creatures which, with a sudden whir of wings, can soar high into the air are often objects of awe and admiration to many early peoples. The cult of the serpent, the only animal without feet or wings, a creature of earth and of water, was more widespread in antiquity than the cult of the dove, although the latter also had its place in man's regard. In Minoan religion both were the familiars of deity, and both rose from the theriomorphic, or animal stage, to the anthropomorphic, or human stage, and became full-fledged deities in their own right. Yet the differences between them were greater than the similarities and remained so even after both had been absorbed into the greater cult of the Mother Goddess.

The origin of the serpent cult has been sought in the varied emotions that all animals, but especially the snake, are supposed to have aroused in the primitive mind. Early man probably thought that creatures of the wild were stronger, wiser, and more subtle than he, even after he had learned to trap them or kill them to provide himself with food. But in attempting to account for the rise of a serpent cult many things besides man's reaction to the creature must be kept in mind: its swift, gliding motion; its mysterious habit of disappearing suddenly into the ground, as though to commune with the underworld; and its propensity for appearing not only near the houses of the living but near the tombs of the dead. Yet far more important than anything else is the almost world-wide belief that a serpent may be the reincarnation of a member of the family who has died.

So persistent is this belief in rural Greece that vessels filled with milk or other appropriate food for serpents are still brought to the cemetery and left beside the grave of a deceased member of the family. Tales are still current of punishment being meted out to children who mistreat a snake that comes to a rural home. The actions of the visitor are then carefully observed, and the whole family is relieved if the snake bears no ill will.

In some parts of the world the belief in reincarnation in serpent form seems to rest upon the similarity between the backbone of a snake and that of a human skeleton. Before disposal of the body by inhumation or cremation became habitual men would have had ample opportunity to observe this similarity and to draw from it their own conclusions. The propensity for appearing near the tombs of the dead may be easily accounted for by the widespread custom, still current not only in Greece but also in many other parts of the world, of bringing gifts of food to the tomb.

That there did exist in Crete an actual serpent cult has long been an accepted fact. If the Minoans believed a serpent to be the visible embodiment of a member of the family who had gone to the After World its favor would be eagerly sought. They, too, may have observed the similarity between the backbone of a serpent and that of a human skeleton, particularly in those early days of life on the island when disposal of a body in a common charnel house was the general custom.

Whatever the origin of the belief that a serpent was the incarnation of a dead person, its presence near the homes of the living was encouraged in Minoan Crete by the setting out of food and drink. Disheartening, indeed, it would be to a family to find a cup of milk rejected by an illustrious forbear, come in serpent form from below to pay a visit to his descendants and discovering some innovation of which he disapproved: a grandson perhaps wearing a loincloth that was too loose or a granddaughter wearing a short, flounced skirt, when a long skirt had been the fashion in his day. In distress and in anger he might glide smoothly away, leaving behind him an untouched dish.

It is to be expected that, if a serpent is still a member of the family, the food which he enjoyed when in human form should remain his first choice. In ancient Greece barley, honey cakes, cheese, and milk were considered a serpent's favorite food. Folklorists often draw attention to an interesting illustration in sixteenth-century Lithuania of the custom of feeding serpent ancestors. They point here not to the kind of food, however, but to the way in which it was set out for the serpents. At certain times of the year peasants would put food on the family table beside the stove and anxiously await the coming of their visitors. Invoked by prayer and by ritual to appear, the serpents would arrive, glide swiftly up over the fresh cloth that had been spread for them, and devour their food.

This illustration, which is frequently quoted, could be paralleled from other parts of the world. In medieval Lithuania, as elsewhere, if the serpents ignored the invitation and did not come to the table for their food it was considered a bad omen for the household.

The favorite food of the sacred serpent that lived under the Erechtheion and guarded the Acropolis is said by ancient

authorities to have been a honey cake. The two serpents on
guard at the entrance of the cave of Trophonios in Greece
were also fond of honey cakes. People who came to consult
the oracle tossed down cakes before descending into the cave.
Minoan snakes seem to have shared this taste, if a ritual
vessel in the shape of a honeycomb with a snake feeding upon
it can be taken as an indication. Evans once suggested that
the partiality snakes apparently have for honeycombs might
be merely a desire to feed upon the honey grubs tucked
away in the cells of the comb. A search for grubs could
easily be interpreted by onlookers to mean that serpents
possess a "sweet tooth," such as other animals have. When
questioned, he added that he had been unable to secure any
confirmation that snakes have an overwhelming desire for
sweets.

Well-to-do Minoan families provided a special room for
their household serpents. The excavators found rooms in
many private houses that, judging from their unusual furniture, could only have been intended for serpents. The furniture in one room included a low, three-legged table of
terra cotta. It was provided with four wide grooves, each
running from the outer rim toward the center, where there
was a hollow in which a small cup would easily fit. The
family serpents were expected to climb up on the table and,
resting their bodies in the grooves, devour the food in the
cup. What happened if more than four appeared together
may be left for the herpetologist to decide.

In this room were also found a number of terra-cotta
vessels: shallow bowls, curiously shaped hollow tubes, and
some of the small three-inch jugs that Evans called miniature
milk jugs. The shallow bowls may have held food.

The hollow tubes excited a great deal of interest. They
were quite unlike anything else previously found in Knossos.
Some were cylindrical and closed at the lower end. Others
were open at both ends. Each closed tube had pairs of cups

attached to either side, usually two pairs to a side. These tubes are thought to have been ritual vessels belonging to a serpent cult. When wearied, or perhaps annoyed, the family serpent could retreat to the interior of a tube. When thirsty he could find liquid refreshment in the little cups.

The snake rooms found in private houses in Minoan Crete indicate clearly enough that the cult of the family serpent had existed on the island from very early days. In its simplest form the cult must have been based upon the belief that the friendly, mysterious creatures who appeared from their holes in the ground to linger about the house were the visible incarnation of the dead. By the performance of certain ritual acts, by the setting out of food and drink, these members of the house might be persuaded to return from time to time to their former homes.

In this primitive form the serpent cult lasted well into the Late Minoan Age. Its existence during this period is substantiated by the discovery at Knossos in 1930 of a private house in which there was a room furnished with all the necessary utensils for a household cult similar to those of earlier days. Some of these utensils were decorated with coiling snakes, their heads poised expectantly above the rims of the vessels. That this room was the center of family life may be concluded from the movable tripod hearth filled with ashes, which was found there. The family had evidently moved here from their former home, bringing with them embers in a sealed tripod, and had deposited them in the room chosen for the household serpent. The usual ritual vessels had also been brought along. If this is the correct interpretation, and many think it is, then we may safely believe that this room, dedicated as it was to the preservation of the family by the performance of ritual acts pleasing to the ancestral spirits, was regarded as the focus of family life.

The house of the Double Axe had a special room, dedicated to the service of a snake-goddess. It contained among other cult objects a small statue, or statuette, made of fine glazed clay, or faïence. The statuette was that of a woman in the full bloom of life. She was dressed in a short-sleeved jacket and skirt, like the fashionable ladies of the day. Her jacket was tightly laced in front and richly embroidered. Over her full skirt she wore a short, double apron with a spiraling festoon down the front. Her headdress was in the form of a high tiara, purplish brown with a white border. And her only other ornament was a necklace. Her hair, cut short in front as if for a fringe, hung down to her shoulders in the back. Grouped around the figure when it was found were several smaller figures, apparently girls or young women, each dressed in a similar jacket and skirt.

The discovery of these figures in what was clearly a household shrine roused unusual interest, especially because of the strange central figure with the spiraling festoon down her apron. But when what had at first seemed to be merely a decoration on her apron turned out to be festoons of serpents, and the peak of her tall headdress the head and unblinking eyes of another serpent, interest changed to excitement. For the statuette was not merely that of a woman in the prime of life; it was obviously that of a serpent-goddess. Coiled and intercoiled just below her waist were snakes; long, snaky bodies slipped up her arms; and one had coiled its tail around her right ear. There was no doubt about it; the snakes belonged to the Lady and the Lady to the snakes. As the anthropomorphized snake, she is the underworld incarnation of the Mother Goddess, whose powers are wider now than before.

The kinds of votive offerings found in these snake rooms help to explain how the Minoans interpreted the needs of their family serpents and of their serpent-goddess. Food and drink, perhaps only at certain seasons of the year, were among their most important needs. In historic Greece, at the time of the spring festival, the *Anthesteria,* householders set out food and drink for the spirits of the dead who were expected to appear in serpent form. The festival lasted three days, and at its close the spirits were bidden to return to the underworld. It is not known whether this custom formed part of the Minoan ritual.

In connection with votive offerings a recent discovery in the Persian Gulf is interesting. Among the remarkable finds made by the Danish Archaeological Mission on the island of Bahrein, some of which appeared in the *Illustrated London News* for January 11, 1958, are four bowls, each with the coiled skeleton of a snake inside. The bowls were in a first millennium shrine. The votive offerings near the bowls included a necklace of "precious and semi-precious stones." The explorers feel that the necklace (which they assume was an offering to a female deity) and the coiled skeletons may "point to the snake-goddess so well known from Crete and Bronze Age Europe."

Just as the serpent came to symbolize for the Minoans the infernal powers of the world below, so the dove, a winged creature of the air, came to be invested by them with celestial powers.

A first step in religious opportunism might be said to have been taken by the Minoans when a snake tube was changed into a rude dove-cot. This process can be clearly seen in a terra-cotta cult object found on the island of Cyprus, where associations with Crete began at an early period. The cult object is a cylinder shaped like a snake tube but with two holes above and a doorlike opening below just large enough for a bird to enter. The tube either came from Crete or was made in Cyprus by Cretan workmen.

Another snake tube, also found on Cyprus, has a series of holes. In addition, the artist has molded upon the sides of the tube several doves apparently in the act of flying out of the cylinder. The doorway below is larger than the one in the first cylinder, and in it stands a female figure, interpreted by Evans as a dove-goddess. "Strange, indeed," he writes, "is this process of evolution by which a mere section of a Minoan water-pipe—haunt of the common snake—was eventually metamorphosed into the semblance of a dove-cot sacred to a heavenly Goddess."

Evans has offered what seems to be the only reasonable explanation of the origin of a snake tube. He discards the earlier theory of a religious origin and offers instead a practical solution of the problem. The clay waterpipes used in the Minoan drainage system, he thinks, provided the first models for the snake tubes. These waterpipes were built in separate sections and then placed end to end in underground channels, where a great many have been found in their original positions.

Some of these sections, especially where the pipes were laid in soft earth, were equipped with what at first sight were thought to be handles, but which were later thought to be loops through which ropes could be passed to help hold the sections together and keep them from sagging, as they would have a tendency to do if the ground were not solid enough underneath. This reasonable explanation was confirmed when pipes without loops were found in places where no sagging could have occurred.

In the West Indies snakes often make their way through the drainpipes into even well-built houses. This helps to bear out the suggestion that the Minoan drainpipes were actual models for the snake pipes, since the islanders must often have observed that drainpipes, especially those laid in open channels, served during the hot season as temporary shelters for water snakes. The next step would be to provide the reptile with a hollow tube of his own. The habit of feeding the household serpents may already have been well established. The final step would be, then, to equip these tubes or cylinders with cups, devised on the analogy of the looped sections, into which drink offerings could be poured.

His thirst assuaged, and perhaps his appetite, the serpent member of the household could glide contentedly into his tube and give himself over to rest and meditation. The change from snake tube to dove-cot must have occurred so gradually as to be almost unnoticed. The simplest explanation might be that doves took possession of what the snakes abandoned. Or they may even have attacked and driven out the earlier occupants.

The importance of birds as religious symbols has long been recognized. Various theories have been advanced to account for the belief that a winged creature may be the visible incarnation of deity. That the dove cult was very old in Crete is indicated by the discovery of amulets made in the shape of a dove that were already in existence at an early period, some of them even dating from the Neolithic Age. Doves perched upon the head, settling upon the shoulders, or fluttering about a person are interpreted as the dove spirit taking possession of the individual and transforming him into a holy person. The spirit has in very truth descended upon him. In Biblical days the Holy Spirit was seen descending in the form of a dove and alighting upon the shoulder of Christ.

Why the dove, rather than some other bird, should have come to be regarded as the vehicle of divine possession has never been satisfactorily explained. Most, if not all, early peoples passed through a period of zoölatry, or animal worship, but this in itself does not account for the predominance of the dove over the winged creatures. Naturalists point out that doves and pigeons, in modern times at least, are more unafraid of man than are other birds, also that they are among the most amorous of birds. Their amorous nature may be one reason why the Mediterranean people generally connected doves and pigeons, but particularly the dove, with a goddess of love and fruitfulness.

During the course of the excavation at Knossos some clay sealings were found that show doves perched upon the roof-

Glazed Clay Snake-Goddess; Candia Museum, Crete; photograph by Alison Frantz.
(Approximate height, as restored: 13 inches.)

Sacrificial Scene, Hagia Triada Sarcophagus; courtesy of Candia Museum, Crete.

Clay Egg-Stand; Candia Museum, Crete; photograph by Alison Frantz.
(Approximate diameter: 10 inches.)

Miniature Sedan Chair; Candia Museum, Crete; photograph by Alison Frantz.

Late Minoan Pottery; courtesy of Candia Museum, Crete.

Storage Jars; courtesy of Candia Museum, Crete.

Crocus Gatherer Fresco (restored); courtesy of Candia Museum, Crete.

The Blue Monkey Fresco; courtesy of Candia Museum, Crete.

Ivory Bull-Leaper; courtesy of
Candia Museum, Crete.
(Approximate height: 12
inches.)

Miniature Swing; Candia
Museum, Crete; photograph
by Alison Frantz.

The Palace at Phaestus;
photograph by Virginia Garner.

Minoan Script, Linear A
(thought to read *To Demeter*);
Detail of Gold Votive Axe;
courtesy of Museum of Fine
Arts, Boston, Massachusetts;
photograph by
Edward J. Moore.

tree of a house, upon a pillar, or upon an entablature. The presence of the doves is usually interpreted to mean that such objects are under divine protection. A more practical interpretation might be offered if it could be shown that for the Minoans the dove, or rock pigeon as it probably was, played the same part in folk belief that the stork has long played in Teutonic belief. The presence of doves on the roof of a house would then be a good omen for a people to whom children were an economic asset.

Whatever the factors that were involved, the dove early became imbued with divine powers. As with the serpent, which became an object of cult, so it was with the dove. The anthropomorphized snake became the snake-goddess, the anthropomorphized dove became the dove-goddess. A parallel for the latter transformation may be found among several tribes belonging to the lower cultures of Australia, where the eagle hawk is believed to have become an anthropomorphic deity.

Lesser cults tend to be absorbed into the greater; lesser deities, to be absorbed in the greater deity. The serpent and the dove lost their separate identities and became manifestations of the Mother Goddess. Coiled about their divine Mother or perched upon her shoulders, they symbolized her firm control over the world below and the world above. Through them, she was imbued with powers both of the underworld and of the heavens.

CHAPTER ELEVEN

THE MOTHER GODDESS

In the portico leading to the great east hall of the House of the Double Axe a towering, resplendent figure may once have stood, its gold and ivory gleaming in the sunlight. It is easy to imagine throngs of people gathered there, eyes filled with awe, as they gaze spellbound at the tall figure, their divine Lady, the Goddess whom they know and revere. For this glorious statue, whose crystal eyeballs flash in the sun and transform her into a creature aglow with life, is the earthly tenement into which the Mother Goddess may, after due performance of ritual, be induced to come and bless them by making it her temporary home.

People are not sure of the name of their Lady; for she comes to them in many guises and under many names. Some of her people think she is the lightning that flashes across the sky or leaps from peak to peak on the mountain ranges. Others think she is present in the arena, when, to do her honor, her children match their strength and their agility with the bulls. Yet one thing they know, and they renew their knowledge each time they gaze upon the tall figure in the east portico. She is their holy Mother; for them she holds in check the terrors of earth and sea and sky. To her they bring their offerings; for her they perform their dances; clinging to her hand they go to the After World.

This cunningly devised statue of the Mother Goddess, which many feel confident once stood in the east portico of the Third Palace, has long since perished. But Minoan artists and craftsmen have left behind them many varying representations of their deity, and from these one can form some idea of her appearance. Although over the centuries she has changed somewhat to conform to the changing ideas of her people, essentially she has remained the same, a maternal figure, the symbol of eternal Motherhood.

The generally accepted view today is that even in the Neolithic Age the inhabitants of Crete thought of divinity in terms of motherhood. Mother and son rather than father and son formed the center of their religion. Clay figurines of the extremely heavy-buttocked type known as *steatopygous* have appeared in Neolithic strata, one with protuberant breasts and in an advanced stage of pregnancy. Some authorities believe that these figurines are early prototypes of the Mother Goddess. Others point out that, for the most part, these Neolithic images were found in island graves and, as nearly as can be ascertained, in graves where males were buried. According to this theory, their maternal forms can be accounted for only by supposing them to have been gifts to the deceased, to serve him in another world, rather than by regarding them as prototypes of a Mother Goddess.

Just when the conception of a mother goddess rose to the surface of Minoan consciousness is not known. Some students of primitive religion feel that throughout the prehistoric Aegean world all ritual centered in Mother Earth. From the worship of Earth as a sentient being would spring up a vague conviction that individual divine or semi-divine beings existed, each presiding over some particular phase of life. Such beings would be the Lady of the Pillar or the Lady of the Serpents. It is generally true that in time individual cults tend to coalesce into a universal cult that gradually becomes greater than the sum of its parts. The Minoans may never have reached the stage of a final and complete union, but at least one way to account for the apparent contradictions in the cult of the Mother Goddess is to assume that a certain degree of amalgamation and absorption did take place in the later stages of their belief.

The Mother Goddess is sometimes pictured in Minoan art armed with a bow and arrows or carrying a double axe or standing quietly at the foot of a tree, her hair decked with flowers and flowers in her hands, accepting offerings of flowers and of fruits from women. These offerings were probably believed to restore and refresh her powers. Often a priestess is pictured in the act of plucking fruit from a tree; but whether she intends to offer the fruit to the Goddess or whether she will eat it herself and thus receive into her own body its fructifying power is not clear.

The Mother Goddess is always shown wearing the dress of the period, whether she is out hunting or whether she is receiving offerings from her people. For the Minoans were not unlike other early people, who, as soon as they have reached the anthropomorphic stage of religious belief, make the images of their deities in the likenesses of themselves, complete with clothing and accessories.

Minoan artists seldom portray the Mother Goddess alone. At times a lion stands guard over her. Sheep and goats often stand beside her, their young nuzzling against the mother's flanks or peacefully cropping the grass close by. As Lady of the Underworld, she is attended by serpents; and as a celestial being, her sacred doves flutter about her head or perch upon her shoulders. In the After World her griffin sits as judge over the newly arrived souls.

Animals are not her only attendants. A signet ring from

Mycenae and a sealing from Hagia Triada show two young girls, possibly twins, in attendance upon her. Similar maidens appear elsewhere. They are always dressed in clothing which duplicates that worn by their divine Mistress, scaled down to their diminutive stature. One twin offers flowers; another plucks fruit from a sacred tree. To perform these tasks they stand upon piles of rocks. It has been suggested that the maidens who constantly appear with the Goddess show that the cult was essentially feminine.

But male votaries also attend upon the Goddess, if we can trust the interpretation of certain bronze figurines found in the late Shrine of the Double Axes. One of these figurines stands upon a small square base and offers a dove to the Goddess. His dress differs both from the Late Minoan fashion and from the belted tunic worn at this time in Mycenaean Greece. In fact, his costume is almost that of a girl. His sleeved jacket, slit low in front and laced up behind, is tucked into a tight belt that secures his loincloth.

Another figurine shows a youth in a belt and a somewhat scanty loincloth with a flap behind. From under a curious peaked cap his hair falls in curls over his shoulders. Both arms are bent in front of him in the usual ceremonial attitude. His legs are encased in leggings somewhat like those still worn in Crete today. Bracelets adorn his wrists, and a gold wire about his neck keeps his long hair from flying.

Some authorities think that this bronze figure is not an attendant upon the Goddess, but a votive offering. Others disagree with both interpretations. They think both figurines represent the Cretan Zeus as a Boy-god. Pictured in art as a slender, youthful figure, he frequently appears with the Mother Goddess or alone on signet rings, on seals, or on vases. Early legend makes him her Child, sprung from her body without male assistance. He represents the birth of the vegetation and its death, that annual coming to life and decaying which is the vegetation cycle. Each year the Mother is doomed to mourn his passing, for, mortal or at best semi-divine, he cannot escape death. By prayer, by ritual dance, and by fitting sacrifice he may be restored for a brief season to his Mother, only to depart again with the passing of the vegetation, leaving her with the dread fear in her heart that never again will he return. Evans calls her the *Mater Dolorosa* of antiquity.

As an infant, seated upon his Mother's lap, the divine Child receives gifts from those who would adore him. Similar scenes appear on a signet ring from Thisbe (which may be a forgery) and on a late Minoan ring. One is reminded of the adoration of the Magi at the birth of Alexander the Great and at the birth of Christ.

Minoan artists also portray the growth of the Child. An ivory figurine shows a boy, shortly before he has reached puberty, richly dressed in a loincloth made of gold plates. The crown of his head has been shaved, as though the youthful god had undergone ritual tonsure. Probably his head was once covered by a cap, a sort of biretta of gold. A signet ring shows him as an armed god, equipped with shield and spear and carrying a bow on his shoulders. That he is god and not mortal is proved by a small double axe engraved beside him. Summoned by the Mother Goddess, who is also represented on the ring, he floats down toward her from the upper air. On another signet ring the young warrior god comes down to take his place in front of a pillar.

Toward the end of the Late Minoan Age the Boy-god seems to have lost prominence before the slow advance of pro-creative ideas. Instead of a son, the Mother Goddess now has a male consort. This idea, according to many authorities, would have been totally incompatible with the character of earlier Minoan society, in which the true fatherhood of children was either unknown or at any rate not taken into account. Although, in the course of time, the concept of a father and son arose to take its place in religious thought, the parallel concept of a virgin Mother and her Child has never been submerged.

The Mother Goddess is the bringer of life; but she is also the bringer of disease and of death. In the hope of currying favor with her or of averting her displeasure men brought to her shrines all manner of votive offerings. From Petsofá, for example, have come votive offerings in the shape of parts of the human figure, often the whole figure. Clay models of oxen, goats, rams, even of pigs, dogs, tortoises, hedgehogs, weasels, and birds have been found and identified as votive offerings. Who knows what story lies behind each small object? Some scholars hold that the miniature house-fronts are to be classed as votive offerings. Perhaps they were brought to the Goddess as a mark of gratitude for her having saved some Minoan family from destruction.

Locks of hair were also brought to the Goddess. In many parts of the ancient Mediterranean world both boys and girls, when they attained the age of puberty, cut off locks of their hair and offered them to springs or rivers or to the god or goddess they had been taught to consider the protector of their youth. So it was with the hero Achilles. His father promised, when his son should arrive at the threshold of maturity, to offer a lock of his hair to the Spercheios, the broad stream that coursed so proudly through the wide acres of his ancestral land of Thessaly. Destiny willed otherwise, for it was in the dead hand of his comrade Patroclus that Achilles himself placed a severed lock of his hair.

The Boy-god not only had the crown of his head shaved, but his forelock had also been cut off. This, added to other evidence too detailed to be included here, has led scholars to believe that the custom of cutting off locks of hair at puberty and dedicating them to a deity existed in Minoan Crete in much the same form as that found in other parts of the Mediterranean world. Evans has called special attention to a shrine in which two locks carved out of soft stone hang on its rear wall. In a shrine at Knossos similar locks of hair were found, apparently intended to be fastened to the wall.

Lucian writes in the second century B.C. that at the time of a young man's first shaving, the hair from his chin was placed in a gold or silver receptacle, inscribed with his name, and nailed upon the walls of a temple. Lucian adds that the hair from his own chin was disposed of in this way. The custom may have been a refinement upon the earlier habit of fastening offerings of hair directly to the walls of a shrine.

The worship of the Mother Goddess permeated the whole of Minoan life. Conch shells found at Knossos may have been used at a state shrine either for crying out to the Goddess to appear and receive her offerings or for calling the worshipers together. The east hall, near where the statue of the Goddess may once have stood, could have served as a state shrine, although there is no actual evidence that it ever did.

Nor is there evidence as yet that the Mother Goddess was ever worshiped in a cave sanctuary. In most parts of the world when natural caverns were abandoned as dwelling places for the living, they became burial places for the dead, and sacrifices were offered there. Ultimately these caves became sanctuaries. Their sanctity was increased if they happened to have stalagmitic formations, as in Psychro Cave, where the sign of the double axe on the pillars shows that they were thought sacred.

In some shrines the charred bones of animals have been found, in others stone pounders, used perhaps to crush barley into sacrificial meal. A characteristic decoration of many shrines consists of festoons of beads and pendants, looped along the walls or the sides of an altar. Festoons were also hung between the columns of shrines, on the legs of tripod altars that supported ritual horns or double axes, and, as has been shown, on the blades of the axes themselves.

The ritual horns and double axes that occur frequently

in shrines dedicated to the worship of the Mother Goddess sometimes occur together, sometimes singly. An agate intaglio shows a double axe rising from between the horns of a bull's head. The double axe, one is led to think, is the cult instrument symbolizing the actual axe used to stun the animal before the sacrificial knife was plunged into its throat.

Other symbols played a part in the worship of the Mother Goddess. To ward off evil from her, or possibly from themselves, if they incurred her anger, the young girls who attended her wore on their shoulders a large butterfly bow, or knot, similar to the knot that *La Parisienne* wears on her shoulders. The Candia Museum has a good example of this butterfly, or sacral, knot. Its long fringed ends, Evans thinks, may have been gathered into tassels, perhaps with fine gold wire. These sacral knots, which often appear in pairs, are engraved on seal-stones and on signet rings, painted on the walls of houses, or flaunted before a charging bull. They are associated with the double axe, with ritual horns, with sacred trees, and with many other objects of a religious nature. Although they are known only from pictorial art it is thought that the originals may have been made of woven material which could have been easily knotted.

The magical significance of knots was well known in the ancient world and has not been altogether forgotten today. Tying a knot will keep something from happening; untying it will remove a hindrance. Although Alexander the Great cut the Gordian knot instead of untying it, he, too, removed a hindrance. Among the ancient Assyrians a knot was tied, or several knots if the matter was really serious, to prevent the dead from annoying the living. The simplest explanation of Minoan knots might be that they were believed capable of warding off evil or hostile influence, upon the analogy of the ancient belief that if the evil is driven out the good may then flow in.

Sacrifices, libations, dances, and music were a part of the

Mother Goddess's ritual. Bulls and goats were sacrificed to her; libation vessels, mostly jugs with handles and spouts, and low tripod tables with cuplike hollows, have been found in her shrines; dancers and musical instruments appear in scenes that center their interest in the Goddess. The conch, the lyre, the double flute, and the Egyptian sistrum were all known. The little hand bells of terra cotta found in the excavations may have served much the same purpose as bells do today in certain religious services to mark the various parts.

There is some evidence that during the ritual seated votaries passed from hand to hand a chalice of sacred juice. As the chalice made its rounds each votary took a sip and thus entered into communion with the divine essence. That the juice was the juice of the grape seems clear from a scene in which a small maiden is shown in the act of plucking a bunch of grapes to offer them to her Mistress, who is seated beneath the overhanging vines. The religious frenzy characteristic of the ritual dance performed by the votaries in honor of their Goddess may, then, have owed its inspiration to grape juice.

At times the Goddess is depicted holding in her right hand a sword and in her left an object with flowing streamers. Scholars have called attention to the remarkable similarity between this curious object and the *aspergillum* of ancient Roman religion. But the *aspergillum* of the Romans consisted of the hair of a horse's tail attached to a rod. Dipped into water, it served as a holy-water sprinkler and has survived, although in a somewhat different form, in the Christian church today. The object with flowing streamers which the Goddess sometimes holds is believed to have had from an early date a recognized place in Minoan religion. The appearance of this object or wisp, as it has been called, may be conjectured from the remains of a small relief found in one of the earthquake-torn houses. From a round handle projects something that resembles a flat, curved tongue slightly pointed at the outer end. On ceremonial occasions, to signify his spiritual power the wisp may have been held by the Priest-King. To hold both sword and wisp at the same time might then mean that the Mother Goddess had delegated to him both temporal and spiritual power.

The suggestion has been made that the wisp might have figured in baptismal ceremonies. This suggestion is of more than passing interest, although, unfortunately, there seems to be no evidence to support it. Yet the many lustral areas in the royal palaces and in the houses of well-to-do citizens at Knossos may have been intended for some sort of purification ceremony in which the wisp was used.

To signify her association with the sea the shrines of the Mother Goddess are often paved with sea shells and with water-worn pebbles; their walls are adorned with flying fish and with sea spray; pitchers and cups reserved for her are decorated with water creatures and with seaweed, since as Mistress of the Sea all these things belong to her.

The Mother Goddess has a ship in which, if need be, she can transport her sacred possessions across the sea. In the design on the Ring of Minos she steers her ship across the waters. The ship carries two pillar altars, each surmounted by a pair of horns. For when the vegetation dies the Goddess takes her ship from the holy place where it has been kept and goes away over the sea, taking her sacred pillar altars with her. She is guided on her journey by the Boy-god or by her consort, who has come to fetch her. In a scene on a gold signet ring found in a grave on Mochlos the Goddess is arriving at a rocky port. One end of her ship terminates in a dog's head, the other in a fish's tail. On this journey the Goddess has brought with her a throne and a tree. She seems to be just stepping down from her throne and is about to disembark with her sacred tree, which she is transferring from one holy place to another.

These two scenes complement each other, for the Mother Goddess appears in the one as the Lady of the Pillar and in the other as the Lady of the Tree. And if the pillar represents a tombstone and a tree represents burgeoning life, the Mother Goddess is in very truth a nature goddess, presiding over both life and death.

CHAPTER TWELVE

THE MINOAN CULT OF THE
DEAD

Between the city of Knossos and a group of rock chambers
that had been hewn out of the limestone ridges to the north,
flows the Kairatos River, a shallow stream during the summer
months but in winter a raging torrent. Across this river and
up into the distant hills, following a ramp along its zigzag
course, a funeral cortege might have been seen almost any
time, during the fifteenth century before Christ, making its
way toward one of the last resting places of the dead.

To an ancient spectator, watching from the House of the
Double Axe or from a point of vantage in the outskirts of the
city, the sight of a funeral procession might not have brought
any strong feeling of dismay, for the dead man would not
necessarily have become an exile from the family circle. Since
he was no longer able to manipulate his mortal body he
merely needed assistance in changing his temporal residence
for that new home which would now receive him. Here
members of his family would come from time to time to
visit him. They would see to it that he was kept supplied

with food and drink and whatever else he needed for his new life in the After World.

Had he been a man of rank or substance, he would have taken care beforehand to have his new home well prepared, perhaps have superintended the workmen as they hewed it out from the rock, arranged and adorned its inner chamber for him and its outer chamber for his visiting family and friends. His mortal body now encased in gold, a gold death mask snugly fitted over his face, his seal ring on his finger, and a funeral ring suspended from his neck, he could expect to preserve his identity forever. On the floor beside his couch would lie his treasures: the gold cups from which he drank, his finely wrought sword and other weapons, the jewels in which he took delight, all of which he would need in the After World; the bodies of animals slaughtered to provide him with food, and perhaps a human victim or so to provide him with companionship.

Whether even a Minoan man of rank wore a gold death mask, as was common in Egypt, cannot be said with any certainty, since no masks have been found in Crete. But gold bands have been found. And since they resemble somewhat the eye bandages on Bolivian mummies it has been suggested that the Minoan gold bands may have covered the eyes of a dead man, either to protect him against evil spirits or to prevent him from "overlooking" the living.

No one knows how the dead were clothed for the tomb, or whether they were clothed at all. On the island of Ceos, at a much later date, the body was fully clothed before being carried to the grave, but the clothing and the couch that served as a bier were brought back to the house. In very early days collective burial in charnel houses was customary in some parts of Crete; or the dead were thrust into a niche or a deep crevice or, at times, into a cave large enough to hold many bodies. Later, when coffins came into use, a rude form of embalming was apparently the fashion for men of rank. Egyptian records mention chiefs embalmed in oil of cedar "as far as Kefatiu."

In the imaginary funeral cortege just mentioned the male members of the dead person's family no doubt carried him to his tomb. Women may also have formed part of the procession. In Athens, as late as the fifth century B.C., women relatives walked close behind the bier to catch the lingering soul and insure its being reborn into the same family. For in ancient Greece people believed that if the soul had not been safely banished, by appropriate ceremonies, from the house to the underworld, it would follow the funeral procession and try to enter the body of a woman. Therefore women of the right age and relationship had to walk behind the bier to prevent the soul's entering the wrong person.

The Cean burial regulations expressly forbade three things at death: placing a cup under the couch of the dead person; pouring out the water in which the body had been washed; carrying the sweepings of the house to the tomb. This attempt to stamp out long-established practices cannot be fully accounted for. One wonders whether the Cean lawmakers were so advanced as to wish to break down the belief that the soul was a tangible entity and could be caught by any one of these methods. Without literary records it is impossible to say whether any such movement occurred in Crete.

The bodies of young children and sometimes even of adults were placed in a sitting position, knees drawn up under their chins and hands touching their faces, and thrust into earthenware jars or urns. These urns were then generally placed in the earth with their occupants' heads up. It is true that two burial jars with the contracted skeletons of children within them have been found, not inverted, but lying with their openings to the west and the heads of the skeletons facing eastward. But there is no evidence that this was a common or conscious practice. The contracted and crouched position of the bodies in the burial urns may be due to an effort to prevent the dead from moving about and escaping to become malignant ghosts preying upon the living. Whatever the purpose, many of these urns have been found, twelve near Knossos and whole cemeteries of them throughout the island.

A primary duty of the ancient family was to care for the dead. In many primitive communities the living are reluctant to part with members of the family who have died. Hence the custom of house burial, perhaps the earliest kind of burial. Reluctance to part with the dead may have sprung not only from man's inability to believe in the phenomenon of death but in his early recognition of the kinship between sleep and death. If, while a man sleeps, his spirit may wander about, as in a dream, and eventually return, then, although someday he may appear to be sleeping longer than usual, who is to say whether his spirit may not merely be absenting itself longer than usual? If, however, it becomes evident that his body must be disposed of, it is safer to dig a hole in the house floor and bury it there, lest the wandering spirit should return and be angry with the family for sending his helpless body far away.

When house burial was given up for adults, it was retained as the proper method of burial for infants and very young children, perhaps that the spirit of the dead child might return in the person of the next infant born to the house or, as some say, that young children need not be separated from their parents. At Knossos the excavators found a newborn baby that had been buried in a cavity under the floor of a house, presumably the house of its parents.

House burial for infants was the custom in other places besides Crete. On the island of Melos eight jars were found under house floors and on Mochlos fifteen. And at Lerna, Mr. Caskey has found dozens of these burials. In the urns from

Melos the oldest child was just beginning to cut his second teeth.

In Minoan Crete larger receptacles for adult burials gradually replaced urns. These receptacles, shaped somewhat like an old-fashioned bathtub with a raised head, were usually long enough to hold the entire body without the necessity of contracting it. Handles were often added to the sides of these coffins, or sarcophagi, as the Greeks called them. When in a later age rectangular tubs, rather like the modern type, began to be constructed lids were fitted to them and they were used as coffins. Somewhat similar bathtub coffins, with lids of wood and gypsum, have been found by the Danish Archaeological Mission at Bahrein.

And in the summer of 1957 the British School of Archaeology at Athens, while excavating near the Royal Road at Knossos, chanced upon a peculiar type of *tholos,* or circular tomb, hitherto unknown to northern Crete. It was built about 1900 B.C. (the Middle Minoan Age) to be used as a family tomb. Inside the tomb was a bathtub coffin containing fragments of a skeleton. Unlike the Bahrein coffins, the Knossos coffin had no lid. The *Illustrated London News* for February 22, 1958, which published photographs of the excavations, remarks upon the fact, important historically, that this tomb was already in use as a family vault when the earliest *tholos* tombs were being constructed on the Greek mainland.

The bathtub coffin of the Knossos *tholos* and those from Bahrein were undecorated. The sarcophagi, however, were frequently decorated with painted designs. Fish, ducks, and papyrus clumps were favorite subjects. Often the design includes a butterfly, a symbol of resurrection to many early peoples. The sarcophagus from Hagia Triada is profusely decorated in the gayest of colors. There are other indications, too, that to the Minoans death is not the dark and gloomy thing it is in the *Iliad* and the *Odyssey,* where, except for a few fortunate mortals, life in the underworld is pictured as without cheer or hope.

In the large cemetery at Zafer Papoura a hundred tombs of the Late Minoan Age were excavated. None were *tholos* tombs. Some of those excavated were obviously intended for individual burial; others were for more than one person. Scholars divide these tombs into three kinds: chamber tombs or family vaults, shaft graves, and pit graves. Shaft graves and pit graves are generally dug deeper into the ground, with a steeper passageway leading down into them than is found in the usual chamber tomb. One chamber tomb, which had been dug out of the solid rock, held the fragmentary skeletons of three persons, presumably father, mother, and child. Shaft graves and pit graves seem to have been intended for individual burial, although so many had already been looted before the excavators reached them that it is difficult to be certain on this point. Tombs cut out of the solid rock—the best example is the Tomb of the Double Axes—are of great antiquity in Crete, going back to about the eighteenth century B.C. Travelers have often commented on the similarity between these Minoan tombs and the more elaborate type in Egypt, particularly at Beni Hasan. Many tombs in the cemetery at Zafer Papoura were those of the well-to-do, but the majority, to judge from the objects of inferior workmanship found in them, must have been the burial places of the poor.

In the cemetery at Isopata, between Heracleion and Knossos, the excavators found a chamber tomb whose owner belonged to the wealthier class. Although all the tombs in this cemetery bear a certain resemblance to one another, with low, square openings in the sides, possibly for pouring drink offerings into the sepulchral chamber or, according to one theory, to provide the dead person with a window through which, if his eyes were unbound, he could see the sky, this tomb had a high corbeled vault of unusual dimensions. Like almost all the other tombs on the island, it had been robbed of many of its treasures. But enough remained to warrant the excavators in assuming that it might once have housed the body of a priest-king. Chamber tombs, because they were easily entered through a long, sloping passageway, were especially subject to looting. About half of those that were explored had already been rifled. Of the shaft graves about a third had been looted, while of the better concealed pit graves less than a third had suffered. The Tomb of the Double Axe had a sepulchral chamber furnished with a columnar shrine, ritual axes, and vases for libations. The tomb itself was actually cut from the native rock in the shape of a double axe. The shape of the tomb, which belongs to the Late Minoan Age, and the furnishings of the sepulchral chamber afforded sufficient proof of a close connection between the Mother Goddess and the Cult of the Dead.

The unique Temple Tomb, near which in 1931 the gold Ring of Minos was found, had a pair of ritual horns, a small upper temple over the sepulchral vault, and an entrance into the shrine from a roof terrace above, on which flowerpots stood. The walls of the tomb, which still showed traces of their red stucco, were incised with double-axe signs. The tomb also had a pillar crypt about sixteen feet square and a sepulchral chamber cut from the native rock. The masonry throughout the whole tomb was of excellent workmanship, with heavy cypress crossbeams supporting the ceiling above the vault. As the excavation proceeded Evans became more and more convinced that this Temple Tomb had belonged to the royal house of Knossos. It had suffered badly from earthquake and had afterward been looted by robbers. Consequently when the excavators reached the vault they found nothing of value left. Even the sepulchral chamber itself had been stripped bare.

Proof that an earthquake had occurred came from the pillar crypt. Here a few decayed bones of human beings still remained. Evans imagines that a memorial service in honor of the dead was being held when the catastrophe occurred. The discovery on the roof terrace of small milk jugs identical with those of the serpent room in the House of the Double Axe indicated that sacrifices and offerings were made in tombs both to the spirit of the dead man, who was perhaps thought to return in serpent form, and to the Mother Goddess.

The Minoan cult of the dead seems to have been based upon the feeling that, if a deceased member of the family is treated with due respect, he will become a kind and powerful guardian of the living. Hence everything possible must be done for him, not only to enable him to survive in the After World, but to keep his good will during his sojourn there. To this end he must be kept supplied with all the needful things of life on earth.

But food and drink are not enough for the After World. In the Elysian Fields, Orion hunts the wild beasts with as much zest as when on earth. For this he must have his spear, his bow, and his swift arrows. So it perhaps was in Minoan Crete. A man needed his spear. A woman needed her distaff. A sailor needed his boat, and a lyre player needed his lyre. A child, too, if it had not been weaned, needed its feeding bottle; an older child, his playthings; if a boy, his knucklebones and flint knife; if a girl, her doll and her bone needle. And also, just as adults were expected to enjoy in the After World what they had enjoyed in this one, so young children were expected to enjoy their own small possessions which they were permitted to take with them into their new life.

Such essentials, buried whole or in miniature with their owners and dug up centuries later by the skillful hands of archaeologists, have afforded much incidental knowledge about a long-vanished way of life as well as a fuller awareness of the way of death on the island of Crete.

CHAPTER THIRTEEN

THE GRIFFIN'S COURT IN
THE AFTER WORLD

By one of those strokes of luck that sometimes fall to the lot of the archaeologist and do much to raise his often flagging spirits, a solid gold ring of unusual design and workmanship came one day into Evans's possession. A Greek peasant, digging in his vineyard near the village of Kakovatos in the Peloponnesus, turned up the ring with a spadeful of earth and took it home with him. Knowing only that the ring was gold, but with no notion that it might be of even greater value, he kept it concealed and upon his death bequeathed it to his son. Later on the son sold it to the owner of a neighboring vineyard.

The village of Kakovatos is near the site of ancient Pylos, where Mr. Blegen recently discovered the Palace of Nestor. The *Iliad* knows Nestor as the "grand old man" who, at the time of the Trojan War, had already outlived two generations of men and was still ruling in the third. The *Odyssey* pictures the astonishment of the youthful Telemachus, come to Pylos to seek news of his absent father, when he saw the grandeur

of Nestor's palace. Today one can understand his astonishment, for the tablets found there have disclosed that Nestor
was a prosperous king and that his large establishment was
built up on slave economy: men, women, and children who
had been carried off in large numbers from neighboring islands, including Crete.

That a gold ring had become the property of a Greek living
at Kakovatos could not remain long unknown. Inevitably the
news drifted to Evans. After some haggling over the price
he managed to secure the ring. To hold in one's hand a ring
that a king may once have owned is of romantic interest
to everyone. To Evans the romance was heightened not only
by the possibility that Nestor might once have owned the
ring but by the unusual design on its bezel. Examined under
the microscope, both the design and the fine craftsmanship
pointed to the assumption that the ring was of Minoan origin
and that it must have belonged to a man of kingly rank. So
Evans named his new possession the Ring of Nestor.

Careful study of the design convinced Evans that it could
be interpreted as an artist's conception of the Minoan After
World. The ring itself, he reported, was probably intended
as a funeral signet ring, to be suspended from the throat or
neck of the dead person. He came to this conclusion partly
because the hoop is far too small to fit the finger of either
a man or a woman, partly because of the character of the
design.

The design shows what Evans calls the Griffin's Court. It
is presided over by a winged creature with the body of a
man and a crested, eagle-shaped head. This hybrid creature
is the griffin-judge. Before the throne upon which he is
seated two griffin ladies stand, each with a similar crested
head. Behind the throne stands the Mother Goddess.

The court itself is in the lower part of the design. To make
clear his conception of the After World, if we accept Evans's
interpretation, the artist has divided his field into four parts.

The upper two present separate scenes, but the lower two merge into each other to present one continuous scene: the Griffin's Court. The separate parts of the design are pulled together into a whole by the presence of a great tree with gnarled roots and with thick, leafy branches which, projecting horizontally from the trunk, provide shade for the court. One is reminded, almost inevitably, of Yggdrasil, the great ash tree that in Norse myth supports the world. In the left-hand corner of the upper part of the design the Mother Goddess and a female companion appear. Over the head of the Goddess are engraved butterflies, recalling the symbol of resurrection on the Hagia Triada sarcophagus, and chrysalises, also symbols of resurrection to many early peoples. Behind the Goddess stands a youthful couple. A winged griffin lady beckons them forward. From their expressions and their attitudes of pleased surprise Evans feels sure that this scene represents a young couple reunited in the After World after having been separated by death. He also feels that the young wife came first and her husband afterward.

In the upper right-hand corner crouches a lion with two small maidens, apparently his attendants. Although the lion sometimes appears in Minoan art as a guardian of the Mother Goddess, in this scene he is the warder, like the Greek Cerberus, of the entrance to the After World. Above his head spreads a canopy of leafy ivy, with which the ideas of light and warmth are associated.

The remaining two scenes, both in the lower part, form the Griffin's Court proper. Before the throne of the eagle-headed judge the two griffin ladies lift their hands in the usual attitude of respect. They wear the short, full skirts and low-cut bodices fashionable in their day. They are hostesses, court attendants, perhaps. Evans imagines them as having just warded off an intruder and waiting now for permission to present the newly united young couple to the griffin-judge.

The design taken as a whole may show what the Minoans

believed, or at least hoped, would happen to them when they arrived in the After World: a happy reunion with their loved ones and a joyous life patterned on the life they had left behind. The ladies would dress like those who presented them at the Griffin's Court, in the gay reds, blues, and yellows they loved so well on earth, and the gentlemen would continue to be their companions. Surely nothing better than this could man desire for the afterlife of his soul.

Did Minoan man conceive of death as continued existence in bodily form? Did the whole man then arise? Or did his soul at the onset of death escape from his body and make its way to the After World, to stand before the piercing eyes of the griffin-judge? Or did the soul put on a new body? These are hard questions, and no answers can be given to them. But the design presents a little more information concerning Minoan belief in a future life.

The butterflies and chrysalises above the head of the Mother Goddess are not mere decoration. The butterfly symbolizes the soul of man and the chrysalis his outworn body. For the belief that a man's soul in butterfly form flies out of his mouth at the moment of death is a very old one. The Burmese are said to believe that when a mother dies, leaving behind her a young baby, the infant soul in the shape of a butterfly follows that of the mother. If the butterfly is not quickly caught the baby will die.

In historic Greece the identification of the butterfly with the soul inspired Greek art to represent Psyche either as a butterfly or with butterfly wings. The identification still persists in Crete today, where the local name for a butterfly has the same root as the ancient word for soul. And in rural parts of Crete the belief is still prevalent that butterflies are "little souls."

The connection between the butterfly and the human soul is further illustrated in a scene on a Greco-Roman sarcophagus in the Capitoline Museum in Rome, although here the butterfly does not symbolize the departure of the soul from the body but its entrance into the body. In the scene Prometheus, in Greek legend the creator of man out of clay, stands before the goddess Athene. He holds out toward her the inert form of a child and watches intently while the goddess places a butterfly on the child's head. The gesture has been interpreted to mean that the goddess is endowing the child with the breath of life.

The discovery of a minute pair of scales in the Third Shaft Grave at Mycenae points to a possible Minoan belief in the weighing of souls in butterfly form. The scales were made of gold and decorated with butterflies drawn in with fine-incised lines. The interpretation rests upon the Minoan artist's habit of indicating upon an object the use for which it is intended.

It might be concluded, then, that in early Cretan belief the first faint glimmerings arose of a concept that was to exert a deep influence upon future thought. Even as a butterfly emerges from its chrysalis to test its trembling wings in their first upward flight, so the soul of man emerges from its earthly shell and sets off on its journey to the After World. That the Minoans may also have believed in the weighing of the soul, when it finally appeared in the Griffin's Court, is equally significant, since it suggests that Minoan religion like the Egyptian, where the soul was thought to be weighed, had its moral and ethical side.

The design on the Ring of Nestor does not make clear where the Minoans located the court, nor is information forthcoming from any other source. Whether they thought of it as under the earth or in some vague region toward the extreme west, a notion that still survives in many parts of the world, cannot be determined.

The young couple who have just arrived in the Griffin's Court are about to be presented to the griffin-judge. Whether each is now expected to give an account of his previous life it is impossible to say. But if this is part of the artist's conception of the After World and if he has based his conception upon the actual belief of the people, that the soul after death must be brought to judgment, then Minoan religion over thirty-five hundred years ago introduced to the Western world a concept of profound significance.

CHAPTER FOURTEEN

THE DOWNFALL OF THE HOUSE

An artist of the Middle Minoan Age, if permitted by the griffin-judge to revisit Knossos during the fifteenth century B.C., would have observed a change in the decorative designs on the frescoed walls of the great palace. The wild rose and the lily, so frequently a source of inspiration to artists of his own day, would no longer have delighted his eyes. Nor would he have found them painted on the Priest-King's vases or on the gold pendants that often adorned the jeweled necklaces worn by the queen and her ladies. Had he asked what had happened to the lily and to the wild rose, with its delicate petals and clinging tendrils so admirably adapted to the artist's brush, he might have received only a puzzled stare in reply. Today archaeologists could do more than look puzzled; for they have learned the fate of these flowers. Centuries ago, they would say, deforestation set its mark upon the island, and the springs that once supplied the House of the Double Axe were slowly reduced to a mere trickle. The trees were forced to retreat to the hills; and the lily and the rose bloomed no more.

In earlier days both flowers had often appeared in frescoes, on ritual vessels, on tall jars, and as offerings to the Mother Goddess. A group of Madonna lilies, painted on the dark red plaster of a wall in a private house in Knossos, is only one of the many examples of the use of these flowers by Minoan artists. Nothing similar to it in beauty or in fidelity to nature was discovered again during the entire excavation of Knossos. The water lily, too, gradually disappeared from decorative art.

Although the fresco painter, the vase painter, or the craftsman whose cunning hand had fashioned many a jewel for a Minoan lady could not have known what the archaeologists have learned, a Minoan architect might have given a partial answer. For, as the excavators peeled slowly back layer after layer of the centuries-old fill that had buried the site, they found that in the earlier buildings timber had been freely used for beams and pillars, and that then stone had gradually begun to take its place. They noticed too that the stone pillars were shaped like tree trunks but set upside down, creating a top-heavy effect.

As the excavations progressed and more top-heavy columns were unearthed they concluded that in the beginning Minoan builders had used the trunks of trees to support the floors and ceilings of each palace. To keep the trees from continuing to grow they set them upside down and so produced a top-heavy appearance. Then as timber grew scarcer and native stone had to be substituted, later architects followed the pattern already set, and the top-heavy column came to be a characteristic of Minoan building.

In any country a timber shortage may prove to be serious. To an island that depends upon wood to build its ships such a shortage, unless it is checked or compensated for in some way, may easily become a major disaster. That the

Minoans compensated somewhat for their shortage by importing cedar from Lebanon is evident from Egyptian records which mention Minoan "vessels of cedar-wood." In the fifteenth century, B.C., Thothmes III, the ruling Pharaoh, wanting the same kind of wood, commissioned Minoan captains to bring it to him from Lebanon, doubtless that he too might have in his navy "vessels of cedar wood." For a time, then, the importation of cedar may have helped to make up for the shortage of timber.

In Crete the Late Minoan Age was an era of industrial expansion. International relations were also cemented. Ships improved steadily. Round cargo ships, like the one the ill-fated Scylla had clung to so desperately, gave way to slimmer and speedier vessels, better adapted for chasing pirates out of the sea lanes. The rudder was lengthened; two or even three masts appeared; a deck was built over the heads of the rowers; and a fighting ram was added to the prow. Wood and more wood was constantly needed; yet the native forests were being exhausted.

Clever though they were in other ways, the Minoans could have known nothing of the comparatively modern science of reforestation. Their only recourse, even had they been aware of coming events, would have lain in prayer and ritual dance before their divine Mother, under whose nurturing care they felt that all vegetation renewed its life. They had always turned to her when the fruit-bearing trees were nearing their end and the deciduous trees had begun to shed their leaves. They must also have turned to her for the pine, the cypress, and the palm. Yet deforestation went steadily on.

No archaeologist, however rash, would be willing to ascribe the fall of Knossos and its royal House entirely to deforestation. Still, he would be willing to admit, with Evans, that a growing timber shortage must have been one of the causes, and an important cause, of the passing of Minoan power into other hands. But ambition played an equally important part.

The ambition of these ancient sea lords of Crete brought ever increasing trade. Trade brought ever increasing population, for people came from far and near, lured by Cretan wealth. But new people meant new houses, and houses needed timber. And new trade meant new ships, and ships needed timber. The great fleet that finally came into being was able, because it could police the seas as it carried cargo from port to port, to make Knossos the seat of the first maritime empire the Mediterranean had known. But the achievement carried with it the seeds of weakness. Steady expansion, the constant acquisition of new markets overseas, could not go on indefinitely if timber for ships failed. Depletion of natural resources carries with it its own punishment. And perhaps the seizing of new overseas markets carries with it another punishment—the hostility of those from whom the markets are wrested. At the peak of her achievement Knossos reached the brink of her fall.

Excavations conducted on the island of Melos, lying to the north of Crete and directly in the path of ships sailing to Greece, have provided enough evidence to link together the civilizations of these two islands. The town of Phylakopi, for example, from which rich finds have come, was laid out on the same block system as that of Minoan Crete. The same type of well-constructed drains also existed, undoubtedly the work of skilled engineers who could only have come from Crete. It may be that Minoan conquest and colonization took place in Melos at a time when the civilization of Crete had reached its zenith in the Late Minoan Age. To this period has been assigned the exquisite Flying-fish fresco, obviously the work of a Minoan artist.

Minoan expansion and colonization by peaceful methods or by force of arms did not stop at Melos. The mainland of Greece continued to beckon, and the islands provided, as in earlier times, convenient steppingstones. Although the excavations on the Greek mainland and on Crete have shown

that a connection between Crete and Greece existed from
Neolithic days, it was not until Crete had gained complete
control of the Mediterranean that the full force of her influence upon the northern mainland began to be felt.

In the Peloponnesus the hill cities of Mycenae and of
Tiryns had already taken shape at the hands of a new, energetic people from the north, the warlike Achaeans. Stone
palaces crowned their heights; their lower slopes were alive
with lesser folk whose small houses clung to the steep rock.
Although the Achaeans had never before laid eyes on the sea,
migrating, as they had from as far north, probably, as the
steppes of Russia, they soon learned the art of navigation.
Raids on land and on sea now took them to far places. It
was inevitable that one day they should descend upon Crete.

But meanwhile Minoan ships plied steadily from port to
port, making better known from year to year the customs of
the Minoan people and their riches. Their island products
led the way, and their people followed. Until recently it has
been widely held by students of the period that Minoan influence so carried soon rooted itself deeply in the life of the
Peloponnesus. In Mycenae, it has been asserted, Achaean
ladies eagerly adopted the low bodice and the flounced skirt,
much as Athenian ladies fetch home Paris fashions today.
The rude Achaean lords became civilized. They adorned their
palaces with painted frescoes and their ladies with necklaces
of amethyst and other precious stones. Only in dress did they
remain unchanged. The gaily striped loincloth of the Minoan
male was not for them.

Now, however, the excavations at Pylos have overturned
this theory of Cretan history and have confirmed the belief
always held by some scholars that Cretan influence spread to
the mainland after Crete had been invaded from the north.
It would seem from the new excavations that about the
middle of the Late Minoan Age the Achaeans came down from
Mycenae, invaded Crete, and brought about the destruc-

tion of her wealth and her culture, particularly that of Knossos.

Knossos had become vulnerable. Not only was she, it might be said, overexpanded (through constant building of ships, seizure of foreign markets, spreading herself too thin for her own resources), but she was, it may well be believed, the object of jealousy at home, since Phaestus and Gortyn, especially, could not have looked with favor upon this rapidly growing power to the east. She may even have been the victim of internal revolution; and she may, indeed, have set a fire to fight a fire and warred on the neighboring cities herself.

In this connection a striking change in decorative design is significant. It occurred in the Third Palace. The time of its occurrence is about the middle of the Late Minoan Age, when a severe earthquake had been followed at Knossos by a period of intense rebuilding. In this period of reconstruction the tranquillity of the earlier scenes in decorative design was superseded by warlike parades. The change may mean the arrival of new and more aggressive rulers from overseas or perhaps a sudden recrudescence of royal activity that was responsible for the destruction of the rival cities on the island.

About this time there was a break in palace history, either a dynastic change or a change in policy. The change synchronized with the earthquake, which was apparently followed by a great fire, and possibly with an internal revolution. As evidence of a fire some scholars point to the smoke marks on the west façade of the palace that Minos Kalokairinos and Stillman had been the first to see. One wonders whether the powerful Priest-King was attacked now by Achaean raiders from overseas and if the attackers were helped by islanders who staged a revolution at home.

If the fifteenth-century Cretan was as fiercely independent in Minoan days as when, over three thousand years later, he finally threw off the Turkish yoke, he might have rebelled against the yoke of the priest-kings. Perhaps he balked at the fetters of social discipline laid down by the ruling Minos and at last disavowed his earlier belief in a system of social legislation based on divine sanctions.

Or perhaps he had simply become weary of being a beast of burden. Look again for a moment at the fortresslike building, the magnificent House of the Double Axe, century after century made more secure against attack. Look at the huge blocks of stone that went into its making. Deep trenches, too, had to be dug in the ground for the safekeeping of the Priest-King's store of olive oil and other treasures. Seventy-nine thousand gallons could be kept there at one time.

The priest-kings had no bulldozers, no cranes for lifting and swinging into place blocks of stone weighing a ton or more. But of human backs there was an unending supply. Perhaps the human back at last rebelled, straightened up, and attacked its master, grown cruel and tyrannical and possibly decadent.

Pasiphaë, the psychopathic wife of Minos, once fell in love with a bull, men might have whispered into each other's ears, and when her time came she gave birth to an ill-formed creature, half man and half bull, housed now in the depths of a fortress made of stone. Why should they labor for such a creature and perhaps be thrown to him in the end? And nowadays the women of the House were no longer what they used to be. They dressed differently in the old days.

Imagination, yes, but social historians often say that the seeds of decadence are to be found in a civilization that has reached its prime. Women's fashions, they say, sometimes sow the first seeds. A fifteenth-century lady, some of the frescoes show, drew her richly embroidered skirt closely around her hips; she painted her lips and exposed her breasts; she flaunted her airs and graces, her jewels, too, in the front seats of the theater, while the men stood behind. At home she leaned far out over her window sill to chat with passers-by. Unfortunately, although the archaeologists have found the faces of the *Keftiu*, they have found no voices to tell us whether the social historians are right or wrong.

It is now accepted as fact that about 1400 B.C. a severe earthquake occurred and that Knossos was attacked and overthrown at approximately the same time. That the catastrophe came as a complete surprise is based upon the discovery of broken ointment jars, with traces of oil still plainly visible, lying in the royal antechamber. This find makes plausible the suggestion that the Priest-King had been rushed from his hall to be rededicated as the head of his people, in a desperate attempt to invoke the aid of the Goddess.

Perhaps the Priest-King had risen too often from his dinner table, well fed and complacent, to mingle with his nobles and their bejeweled ladies in the great hall, where spears stood neglected against the walls and leathern shields had gathered dust. In the hour of danger, as quake after quake sent walls crashing down, his nobles may have tried to anoint him with sacred oil and then offer him as the supreme sacrifice to the Mother Goddess, that by his death they might be saved.

Were the enemy already inside the palace, seizing its women, plundering its treasures, and setting fire to whatever would burn? Or had the earthquake—this time the roaring of the bull was exceptionally loud—frightened them away, to return later for more looting? It is said that the great palace, after having been almost continuously occupied for nearly seven centuries, fell in a single day, a spring day when a strong south wind was blowing. The disaster was complete, for destruction enveloped the whole island. No longer is the name *Keftiu* found in Egyptian records. On the island new people appeared, a broad-headed people who spoke a strange tongue and had little reverence for the Minoan Goddess and her sacred rites.

Though it was the Achaeans whose descent on Crete brought about the major destruction of her wealth and her culture it may not have been they who first broke in on her expanding prosperity, and it was not they who completed her ruin. While she had been extending her trade with Egypt, Asia, and Europe and establishing footholds for further ventures overseas, the Peloponnesus had been disturbed by waves of invasion from the north. Some historians speak of three successive invasions, first by the Ionians, then by the Achaeans, then by the Dorians. These historians believe that the Ionians, not the Achaeans, first crossed to Crete, plundered her cities, and traded with those Cretans who survived their raids.

But if the Ionians were the first to break in on Crete they were soon routed by more successful invaders from the north. For the warlike Achaeans drove them from Crete and established themselves firmly there, overwhelming the Cretan civilization. And after them came the Dorians.

The conquest of Crete by the Achaeans has been compared to the conquest of Greece by Rome; but the arrival of the rude Dorian tribes from the wilds of Albania is comparable to the fall of Rome and the lapse of that great civilization into the turbulence of the darkest Middle Ages. From that darkness the Renaissance awoke the rest of Europe. But for Crete there was no Renaissance. Yet Crete, though conquered and overthrown by the hordes from the north, has continued to live a transmuted life, for she has passed on, through Greece, her arts, her laws, and, to some extent, even her religion to the rest of Europe and, ultimately, to the whole of Western civilization. For this gift the world owes her a debt of gratitude.

To the casual visitor of today who comes by public bus or private car from Heracleion to Knossos, the ruined palace of the Priest-King may seem only a labyrinth of jumbled walls and corridors. But to the dreamer and the poet, Minos the

Priest-King, his spear in his hand, his plumed crown on his head, and his sacred griffin by his side, still walks in his field of lilies. And to the scholar and the historian, the Priest-King's Knossos is one of the great discoveries of the ages, the record of a magnificent civilization which, under the aegis of the Double Axe, flourished thousands of years ago on an island in the Great Green Sea.

A3